# Dragons &
# Butterflies

Trevor Tacey

*I dedicate this book to all those that find themselves trapped in an addiction or some other mental health condition that is a result of an unresolved trauma and they are convinced there is no escape.*

*To my late parents that I now know loved me. They gave me the tools I needed for my journey and some that I didn't need but thank you anyway.*

*To Graham, my youngest brother that left too soon.*

*To my children, who continue to teach me the lessons of life and make me proud every single day.*

*To Alan, my brother who has shown that he also has our mother's courage and tenacity in his own struggles with medical procedures and surgeries over the last four years. You are my hero.*

*Last but not least to Cindy, who together with Alan got me started on this journey. I owe my beautiful wife so much and I have no doubts that without her I would not be sat writing this dedication. Our children wouldn't be where they are in their lives without her loving nurturing nature. I thank God she never gave up on me and I cherish her loving kindness. She was put in my life for a reason and I was blessed that day.*

*Trevor Tacey*
*November 2020*

# CONTENTS

# 1
## NO ONE ELSE CAN TELL IT

My first memory as a toddler under two was standing alone and frightened in the dark and it was snowing. I wonder, was this a clue to what lay ahead of me? At times in my life it almost felt as if I was back there with this feeling of being out in the cold and alone in the world. Were these feelings following me about?

I was just a child and could have no idea of the avalanche that was about to hit me and how I would be pulled back up to the surface by other people and my own desperate scrambling. The first half of my life was going to be an endurance test not just for me but my loved ones too; the second half a series of difficult transitions, transformations and then the healing... a process that is still in progress.

This is my story; no one else can tell it. A good friend once said to me that "his story" was worse than anyone else's because he had to live through it! I knew only too well what he meant by this.

My story is about a journey through trauma, years of addiction and then finding recovery. The main reason for this book is to show that not only can adversity be overcome but we become stronger people as a result of it. That in turn can lead us to reach heights that we could only have dreamed of in the past. We can free ourselves of the shackles that have tied us down for years and rise above it all and know the truth of who we really are.

At least my children and grandchildren will know everything about me, warts and all. Some of it is far from pretty. I didn't know anything really about my parents. This is my chance to be completely honest about my life and where it went. I won't be hiding anything from anyone, especially in this book.

Frightened, alone and in the snow; this is my most vivid memory of my earliest years. We lived in a place called Tomlinson's Yard in Newark; a series of terraced houses built in an L shape going straight up and to the right, maybe thirty houses. Our house was at the top of the straight and that night I had woken up alone in the house and wandered outside looking for my parents. They must have heard me crying because they came out of the next-door neighbour's house and picked me up and took me inside. They were watching a black and white television. Not many people had one in those days in 1952. Although I couldn't have been much more than 18 months old, I can remember a small room, my parents and two other people, a roaring fire and a programme on the television with a dog in it. It was warm and cosy but it was that feeling of being alone, frightened and abandoned that stayed with me. There was something else in that memory that stayed with me too and that was the dog on the television was hurt and had a bandage around its middle and even though I was so small, I felt sad that the dog was hurt. I never understood why it is still so vivid to me all these years later.

I don't know how long we stayed at Tomlinson's Yard but I have vague memories of playing with other kids and being happy. We then moved to Spring Gardens and life was good. I had a garden to play in and I must have had a brother- Graham- by that time but I can't remember him yet. What I do remember is being at the infant school on

Victoria Street and standing at the side of the road with the rest of the school and the teachers as a circus went by on its way to the main park on the edge of town. I was so excited and mesmerised by the sights, sounds and smells of all the animals. These were animals I had only heard about. Elephants walking down the road behind each other, cages with lions and tigers in. They were so close you could see and smell them, strange smells. Hearing them roar was just amazing. I was so excited, fascinated and a little scared at the same time but I never once took my eyes off them.

Things were about to change. I was now old enough to join the junior school and moved into the Catholic school on Parliament Street which was only around the corner, but so different from the infant school where I was happy. It was run by nuns with one civilian teacher, Mr. McCann. I guess I was five years old by then and I was going to be there for three or four years. It is hard to recall anything good about that school but I am sure it wasn't all bad. I became aware that I was Catholic and had to go to church every Sunday, and study the Catechism every day at school. I endured bullying regularly. Playground scraps were the norm but the worst of it was how cruel the nuns were and how they would hit us with the edge of the ruler across our knuckles, grab the hair near our ears and pull both sides at the same time until we cried. Sometimes it seemed as if they almost enjoyed being cruel. Even at this age I was questioning religion in my head because it didn't add up with what I was being taught.

One day when I came back from school after another bullying my mum had finally had enough and promptly took me into the back garden and taught me how to fight. I can remember her on her knees teaching me how to stick up for myself. She gave me a few weekly lessons and I eventually got the hang of it, to the point where I started winning a few fights.

I received my first Holy Communion while I was still at that school and went on to become an altar boy and at that time the Mass was all in Latin. I had to learn the Latin responses during the Mass and I think my mum was proud of me at that time but in the vestry after the service had finished and the priest had left, we altar boys would have a sneaky taste of the wine. After all this wasn't any old wine, this was holy wine!

I only have one bad memory of anything that

happened in the house at Spring Gardens and that was while playing in the back garden I injured my shin on a rusty nail that had been sticking out of a piece of wood. It must have been quite serious because I can still see the scar to this day. Anyway, I wasn't taken to hospital and every week I would be held down kicking and screaming as my parents bathed the scab off with warm water and TCP. This wound was quite wide and ran from just below my knee to just above the ankle and it seemed to take them forever to clean it. I am sure it was needed, but for years the smell of TCP made me feel sick and I would go into a blind panic if anyone tried to pin my arms down, even if it was only in fun or a game.

While I was still at this school we moved again to a public house called The Horse and Gears. I am not sure what my dad was doing at this time because he had worked at a local maltsters at some point, and then at the local egg packers' factory on Millgate. By now I suspect he was running the pub full time with my mum. I was still at the Catholic school on Parliament Street with the church attached to it and classrooms around the back. Life was still mostly miserable there and I was never happy at that school. I had some friends; Paul Kimberley, Ted Marum, and Richard Boyle were my best friends, and I had learned to fish. There were a few of us that would go together to the local rivers after school and I remember that these were the happy times and a pastime that I still enjoy today. We would visit a place called Queens Sconce that was a park but also it was a historic place where we knew battles had taken place in the past. Next to this park was an area of scrubland with a pond in it that was alive with wildlife and we would often visit it after school to catch frogs. Some of these frogs seemed enormous to us and we called them 'bullfrogs'. We were only six or seven at the time, so I am not entirely sure if they even were giant frogs! 'Sconnies' as we called it was one of our favourite places to play, with its swings and slides, trees, and hills. It also had a small pretty river winding through it with lots of yellow water lilies in the summer. It was called the River Devon and it also had some big fish in its murky depths that we would spend hours trying to catch.

There was also a Scout hall just up the road from us, and my mum took me along to join the Cubs. It was in an old church building that smelled fusty. I liked being in the Cubs but for some reason it didn't seem to be for long. It might have been because we moved again.

One thing that sticks in my mind from that time was that my dad gave me a little pocket knife. It wasn't like any of the knives that the other Cubs had. This one was a small gold coloured pen knife with red, yellow and green jewels in it. It was special to me; even more so because it had been my dad that gave it to me. It is strange that this is the only thing I can remember him giving me.

It was around this time that I also found a way to keep the bullies off my back. I became a thief! I found that my parents would leave jars of coins under the bar that held half crowns and other silver. I would sneak down in the dead of night and steal one or two and then go out of the house and hide them away from the house. That time from when I sneaked out of bed, stole the money, hid it and got back home and into bed without being caught was so frightening but it was the only way I knew to protect myself. The next day I would collect the money on the way to school and buy sweets from the local tuck shop to bribe my enemies so they would leave me alone for a while.

I don't know when my behaviour started to change but that was the beginning of it, I think. I can never remember feeling guilty about stealing the money from under the bar. I would have been seven or eight and by now had two brothers, Graham and Alan. Graham was two years younger than me, and Alan was five years younger.

Figure 1 - The three brothers

It was around this time that I witnessed my dad hitting my mum and I can see her now cowering on the floor trying to defend herself, with me transfixed and too frightened to try to protect her. This wasn't an isolated incident and I would have to witness it a few times. This was also around the same time that I started to get beatings from my dad, too. I can never remember what for.

I do remember one particular night when I had had a good hiding for something and sneaked out of the house with the idea to run away for good. I was on a street that used to have an army barracks on it that was now used to store caravans. I was so cold but determined not to go back home so I ended up breaking a window in a caravan, climbing in and trying to sleep. I was alone and cold again. I was also so miserable and I wasn't even ten years old yet. I am sure I was no angel! I have no idea why my dad was the way he was. I can't remember him ever telling me he loved me and he never hugged me but then again I knew nothing about him really. Don't get me wrong, it wasn't all bad, but sometimes they were the only parts I remembered. I was desperate to please him at times but I had no idea how to do it.

The pub had its own fishing club and my dad was the secretary and a keen fisherman himself. I would go with my dad and the other members of the club to fishing matches and I loved it. We would take food with us, a bus would be organised to take us all, and we would be off to different rivers. I was already getting a taste for adventures and they would always take care of me and make sure I got a prize at the end of the day. These were happy times for me and I looked forward to these trips.

One of my favourite memories of that time is what I now refer to as my 'secret garden'. Opposite the pub was a stone archway between two buildings and as you walked through the archway and down a slope you would enter a derelict garden that seemed massive to us at the time. There was an enormous horse chestnut tree and I remember it so well because it was the first time I had ever seen a red squirrel. The sun was shining on it and it seemed to glow so brightly against the greenery.

This secret garden, and fishing with my friends, and the pub fishing trips were my escape. This is a time where I can remember that I felt happy and safe.

My brother, Graham was old enough to come to the garden with me and our other local friends, a boy and a girl around the same age as us. The boy's name was Peter but I can't remember the girl's name. We had another friend that came with us but he became ill and then died suddenly. Nobody explained what happened and it was just a matter of one day he was there and then he was gone.

I think the garden was a special place to us all. When I think of it now I only remember sunshine and blue skies. It had apple and damson trees and right at the back it had an old lean-to conservatory with a grape vine that was filled with black juicy grapes during those summer months. It also had a pond with frogs, newts and minnows. To me it was Paradise and I spent a lot of time there on my own sometimes, just watching the goings-on in the pond, listening to sounds of all the different birds that seemed to surround me. It was another world, a better world; it was filled with magic.

My behaviours were getting more out of hand at school and eventually I was expelled from that school for pushing another pupil into a sand pit that was full of rainwater. I had seen this lad, David, bending down in front of this flooded sand pit and I thought it would be funny to push him in with my foot and so I did. I don't know why I would think that would be funny? My dad would often say there was something wrong with me, or that I was not right in the head.

It wasn't long after this that my parents took me to what I believe now was some kind of child psychologist. All I remember is this big man standing behind his desk, leaning forward with his hands on the desk and he towered over me as I stood in front of him. He was screaming at me, his face all red and the veins sticking out on his neck, and telling me about how bad I was and what I was doing to my parents. I guess he scared me but this was something I was used to. I don't know why they thought a stranger screaming at me was going to be any different to my dad screaming at me. He was more than capable of looking scary with the red-face-sticking-out-veins-in-his-neck thing.

I was beginning to believe what they were saying about me and there was something wrong with me; "maybe he's right and I am not right in the head!" As I have said, my mum was a devout Catholic and one of her friends had been to Lourdes and brought some of the miraculous water back that was supposedly curing people of all sorts of illnesses. I remember seeing this little bottle of holy water in a plastic bottle in the shape of the Virgin Mary and with my dad's words still ringing in my ears I drank the holy water in the hope it would perform a miracle on me and make me right in the head. I just wanted to be normal. I was about seven or eight years old at that time. Well, alas it didn't work! So I quickly filled the Virgin Mary up with tap water and put her back where I found her. I pitied the next person that used it but you never know!

Somewhere inside me I had started to shut part of me off, I was building a defiant streak in me that was saying, "Fuck you!" These were the same thoughts and feelings I had when my dad was kicking off. I was learning about a way to protect myself. I didn't know it at the time but I was learning how to develop coping strategies to help me get through these times. I didn't feel safe at home and so I would spend as much time as I could with my friends and nature. I didn't feel wanted or loved at home and that hurt and left me feeling angry and wanting to get my own back.

I was about to move to a new school; would this be the answer to what I needed to turn things around?

# 2
## NEW SCHOOL, NEW START

That was wishful thinking....

Well, here I am at my new school. This is a
Church of England school and it was built at
the side of the Newark Parish Church with a
spire that must reach two hundred feet into
the sky with a golden cockerel at the top. It
stood in the cobbled town square where the
markets took place. The school had a large
playground and a playing field at the back, and
the classrooms were a row of single storey
buildings with a covered walkway across the
front of them. The headmaster's office was
the first on the left, followed by about five
classrooms. Also on the left was the main
road and running off it was a road called
Slaughter House Lane, for obvious reasons.
When we went out to play at break times I

would see the pigs and cattle being unloaded and taken into the building, and then I would hear the pigs squealing and I could only imagine what terrible things were happening to them. It was a horrible sound and I would fantasise of ways to rescue them. I hadn't been at the school long before the headmaster, Mr. Bates, was chasing me around his desk with a cane and hitting me wherever he could make contact but most of my time there was uneventful. This was still a junior school and it wouldn't be long before I was moved to the senior school, which was only next door through a passageway in the yard.

Life at home was not improving but there were periods when it felt good. My dad would show me how he would change the barrels of beer in the cellar. The mixture of damp air and beer in this dimly lit cellar with whitewashed walls is still clear to me. I would watch him punch the tap into the wooden barrel with a wooden mallet as it lay on its side. He explained to me how it had to be done with one hard strike or the beer would spill out onto the floor. I loved those moments with my dad but they seemed few and far between and disappeared when I heard his violent arguments with my mum. I can't remember what they were about but they were often enough to make me start to hate him. It was a picture in my mind that I couldn't forget and so every time they argued I had the same picture come up of him hitting my mum and I knew one day I was going to make him pay.

After I moved to the senior school it seemed that this period of school life was easier for me but I don't think the teachers felt it was easy for them. I was learning that humour was a way of being accepted and liked by my peers and so I became the school clown, always fooling around, getting into trouble for it, spending time outside the headmaster's office waiting for the cane. One day the Headmaster congratulated me by announcing "Well done, Tacey! You have come first at something; you have had the cane more times than any other pupil this year" He had said this in front of my classmates, leaving me embarrassed. I reacted by being more disruptive and rebellious. There was no way I was going to be forced into taking my education seriously. My school reports were terrible and this disappointed my parents who would compare me to someone else's child: "Why can't you be more like so and so?" I don't think I let it bother me too much at the time. I had been told often enough that there was something wrong with me so why would I be any good at this school stuff? I just didn't try and that is what was written on my reports:

"Trevor could do better"

"Trevor is lazy"

I was more interested in what happened after school than what happened in school...

I had a little bunch of mates: Gordon, he was our leader; Fred, the gentle giant; Loz, a skinny carrot top, and Stan, blonde hair and quite chubby. We would go on these (what seemed like) great adventures. Swimming in the river or a lake, the blue lagoon, fishing, or long hikes on those summer days. Then my family moved again and it was going to have dire consequences that no one could have foreseen.

We left the pub that had been virtually in the town centre and moved to Lincoln Road where we were surrounded by countryside; we were about to become very free-range kids now. Graham was old enough to come out with us but Alan was about five or six so he didn't so much. It was halcyon days of fishing and collecting birds' eggs. We learned how to take an egg from a nest and put a stone of similar size in its place so that the mother wouldn't abandon the nest. We learned how to blow the egg by pricking each end of the egg with a needle and blowing the yolk out, then we would lay them out in sawdust lined tins and display them to our friends as our pride and joy. Those eggs were laid out like precious jewels with all their different sizes and colours. My favourite was a song thrush; her nest was lined with mud and her eggs were sky blue with black speckles.

We made our catapults and throwing arrows ourselves, we climbed trees and we swam in the River Trent. We swam out to the big John Harker barges and pulled ourselves up onto the deck pretending we were pirates and then ran to the back and dived off- sometimes chased by one of the crew- knowing that a slip could mean getting pulled into the propeller but we did it anyway. We were fearless adventurers climbing the biggest trees for a rook's egg or swimming the widest part of the river for a dare, diving off bridges, swimming near waterfalls.

In the summer when we were not at school we would call round for each other right after breakfast and not come home until it was teatime. During the first week in May the

Agricultural Show comes to town, it is a big affair with farmers from all over the country coming to show off their best livestock and compete against each other. There are lots of other things to see. This is an exciting time because every year two or three of us kids would go to the showground on a Thursday night and find the goat tent. We would help the owners set up for the night and then we would spend the night with the baby goats. I would always remember those nights just curled up in the straw with four or five kid goats around me and a feeling of complete contentment and safety. The owners wanted us to stay with them because it stopped them getting stressed. I am sure I got more out of it than they did. The next morning we were supposed to be at school but we always played truant on that day. The owners made breakfast for us and gave us complimentary weekend tickets for the three-day event that ran Friday until Sunday. We would take our tickets to the main gate and sell them to the public. These are good memories of a special time when life at home was far from happy but saying that my parents never tried to stop me going there and I am sure they knew I was playing truant.

Sometimes we would spend days on end at the

local outdoor swimming pool. I loved it there. It had diving boards, a water slide and a big, grassed area to dry out and sunbathe. It also had a café and we would get cups of Oxo drinks to warm us up. This was a time when Alan and Graham would be with me too. I would keep an eye on them but it was safe there and we had Max, the lifeguard watching over things. Max was the captain of the water polo team and we would stay behind to watch the matches on those summer evenings and if we were lucky Max would pick us out to be ball boys. We would swim to the back of the goals and throw the ball back into play if a shot had missed the goal. I think most of Newark had learned to swim at that pool and Mr Bell, the manager, was such a kind soul and always had time to offer advice and encouragement to us youngsters. I soon became a strong swimmer.

Things at home had changed. My dad was working on the power stations and although there were a lot of new stations being built around us, he was working away from home and just came home at the weekends. This suited me down to the ground. I was usually out at the weekends so I don't think I saw that much of him. This was a pretty good time and my mum seemed happy, although she would sometimes make a list of things I had done during the week. If I had been playing her up, it went on the list and when my dad returned he would call me into the house or catch me when I got home and take his belt off and give me a beating. I usually knew I was going to get it and so expected it and somehow managed to block it out by thinking of our next adventure; it was just a matter of me thinking "Let's get this over with so I can get out and get back to the fields and rivers". My mum seemed happier here. I don't know if it was because my dad was away most of the time or that she had more time for herself after running the pub. She was a hard worker and very house proud, always keeping the house tidy and clean. She loved to bake and would show us boys how to bake too. She would make homemade lemonade and her famous coconut tarts. We always had home-cooked food on the table and the smell of something baking in the oven still brings those happy memories back to me.


Going to church every Sunday was still mandatory and non-negotiable. I went begrudgingly! My dad was not Catholic and the only time I saw him at church with my mum was at a baptism. My mum loved taking us to church. She would get us all tidied up and go in with us, her three boys. I never thought it was fair that my dad didn't have to go and I did. I devised one of my cunning plans and asked Mum if I could go to the early Mass at 8am so that I could get back in time to go out with my friends. She agreed and the night before I would smuggle my fishing tackle out of the house and in the morning take off fishing and escape the boring church service. I got away with it for weeks but eventually got caught out and it was back to the later service with my mum.

I was still doing things that my mum would have had a heart attack over if she knew half of it. For example, my friends from school and I would ride our bikes to a place called Besthorpe Pits, which was a few miles from where I lived. We would fish for bream and use freshwater mussels as bait. When we got tired of that we would go looking for gulls' eggs. They had started to fill in these pits with fly ash, a waste material from the local power station and it would form a crust over the top of the lake that the gulls liked to nest on. We would creep on to this crust not knowing how thick it was, but knowing for sure that if we went through it we wouldn't get out. This still didn't stop us and we always managed to get a couple of eggs.

We were always being warned about the dangers of swimming in the river and now and again we would hear of someone drowning during the summer holidays but we never let it deter us. I had my trusted friends who were just as fearless as I was at that age. Intrepid explorers needed to take risks and we were "intrepid explorers" in the truest sense, but something as a young lad I could never have even imagined was about to happen to change my life forever.

# 3
# IT SHOULD HAVE BEEN THE OTHER ONE

It was a beautiful summer morning and after breakfast, we were off fishing again at our favourite place on the River Trent at Crankley Point close to Winthorpe Village. It was the school holidays so us three brothers and our friend Richard Boyle would spend as much time as we could on the river. We had been the day before and caught lots of fish and so we were looking forward to another good day.

After breakfast, we went to sort out our fishing tackle and Graham couldn't find his reel and so he had to stay behind. Alan and I continued to Richard's house and then on to the river. When we got to the riverbank I opened my tackle box and Graham's fishing reel was in my box. I wanted to go back for him but I couldn't leave Alan with Richard as he was too young, only being seven at the time and so in the end, I decided not to go back. I could never have known what the consequences of that decision would mean and how it would haunt me for years to come.

So it's the end of the day and time to go. We empty our keepnets full of wriggling silverfish back into the river and make our way home. I cross the playing field opposite our house, and see a police car parked outside. I begin wracking my brains as to anything I might have been up to that week. I get through the front door and a sense of dread comes over me. Mum is hysterical and someone is trying to console her. It is obvious that something terrible has happened but I have no clue what it might be. Eventually I am told that my brother Graham had been killed in a road accident. My dad isn't here because it is a weekday and he is still at work. I'm left with Alan who is only seven and I am not sure if he can understand what we have just been told.

It was such an awful time and I remember being immediately washed over with the guilt I felt about not making that trip back for him when I had found his fishing reel; if I had he would he still be alive? I was the eldest, I was the one that was supposed to protect them and I had failed Graham in a way that was unimaginable. I carried that with me for a lot of years and never told a soul. I couldn't tell my parents how I felt because I had already decided that they blamed me. As time went on I learned that he had been clipped by a lorry on a roundabout at the top of the road while riding back from town after doing an errand for our mum. He had hit his head on the kerb and died instantly. Graham wasn't like me; he was quiet and studious and resembled the 'Milky Bar Kid'. He had blonde hair and those round NHS glasses of the time and didn't get into trouble like his older brother, but we still had some good times together.

I had the responsibility of collecting my brothers from school when mum was working and making sure they got home. I think that back then there were a lot of kids like me that had the front door key hanging on a bit of string that you reached through the letterbox for and we were called "latch key" kids.

I think one of the things that bothered me the most about Graham dying was that I was the eldest brother and I felt that I should have protected him. When I took my brothers fishing or swimming at the local pool, I was always told that as the eldest it was my responsibility to look after them and watch out for them. I knew I had failed Graham and there was no one I could talk to about it. Nobody had the slightest idea how I was feeling.

I didn't know it at the time but I was learning that my feelings were unimportant and that I was on my own. There seemed to be plenty of adults consoling my parents, mostly my mum but I felt that I was left to look after my younger brother while the adults got on with their grief. I was also having thoughts that I didn't like but they wouldn't go away. I was blaming my mum for what happened to Graham because not only was he doing an errand for her but he was also using her bike, which was far too big for him. I wonder, now, how many times my mum had thought the same thing. Was she just like me with my guilty feelings and regrets around not bringing that bloody fishing reel back?

The most disturbing thoughts I was having was that I wanted to find out where the lorry driver lived who had killed my brother and I would find a way to kill him! I would spend hours working out how I could do this. I was full of hatred for the man, even though I didn't know him and had no idea what he was going through. I didn't care; I just wanted revenge! I was twelve years old and these thoughts were eating away at me.

It was around this time that I started wetting the bed. This just added to my feelings of being different or inadequate in some way. Sometimes in my half-sleep, I would know I was doing it and the feeling of the warm urine somehow felt comforting but then I would wake up and realise what I had done and feel the shame and humiliation that was added to when my mum saw it later.

My mum and dad were unavailable for my brother and me as they went through their own pain and grief. I felt abandoned and alone with it all and I didn't know what I wanted. When people did ask me if I was ok and say how sorry they were to hear about my brother, I didn't want to hear it or talk about it. It was painful to be reminded of it all and I was trying to keep a lid on it.

Figure 2 - The last photo

After the school holidays, I had to go through
it all again at school. I hated people feeling
sorry for me. I wanted them to act as if
nothing had happened because whenever
Graham was mentioned I would start crying
and or try to stuff those feelings down. It
seemed like it would never end. Once, not
long after it happened, Alan and I were sitting
in a café in town with my mum having a snack
and two ladies on the next table next to us
started talking about this terrible accident
where a young boy was killed. I can remember
my heart sank and I was thinking "Oh no, not
again" as my mum broke down and told them
it was her son. The ladies apologised and tried
to comfort her but all I could do was sit there
watching and feeling so sorry for her. I just

wanted it all to go away.

My behaviour went downhill when I got back to school. I was getting into more trouble and being more disruptive. I was so angry and was getting into more fights. To stop us ending up in front of the headmaster we began to arrange fights after school in a place called the Friary, a little park near the school we were at. It used to attract quite a crowd and I was in quite a few of them and winning more than I lost, thanks to my mum's coaching skills from some years before.

It wasn't long before my antics came to the attention of my dad and he would be wielding his belt again but I was starting to somehow not be bothered so much by the beatings. It was almost as if I went somewhere where he couldn't hurt me. It was what he said that hurt me more. His favourite saying was "You will never amount to anything as long as you have a hole in your arse" and he would say these things with such venom! I really can't remember what I was doing that was making him so angry. Whenever I thought about the things he said and what he thought about me, then that statement about not amounting to anything as long as I had a hole in my arse would ring in my ears. I can remember thinking some years later with a bit of humour that his statement didn't leave a lot of room for manoeuvre!

The arguments between my mum and my dad started to flare up again after about a year after Graham's death and one day I heard my mum say to my dad "The only reason I stay with you is because of the kids". This just added to the feelings of not belonging, feeling in the way, and just confusion!

One day my mum in a fit of rage screamed at me "It should have been you that got killed, not Graham!" Wow! It cut me to the bone and confirmed to me how bad I really was. I know my mum was still hurting and I was not helping, but it shocked me and I started to believe that there was something wrong with me... "Maybe they are right and I am not wired up right in the head?" All this thought did was to make me angrier and even more defiant. I was the black sheep of the family; I was the outcast, unwanted, unloved and better off dead! Underneath all of this, I knew that Graham wasn't like me and he would have made them proud. I didn't belong there and I wanted so badly to get away from them and out of that house.

My brother Alan told me recently that my

mum would quite often say to him "It should have been the other one" when she heard something that I had been up to.

The only time I felt ok was when I was in the countryside, fishing in my favourite spots with my friends or at some other pastime. We had a special fishing spot called Sam's Island but you needed to get there early. It was at a place called Nether Lock and you needed to get across the lock gates before the lock keeper got up and then we could climb down the bank and climb in a moored up rowing boat and fish out of that. We would catch lovely Perch. They always reminded me of being the gladiators of the fish world with their spiny dorsal fins, spikes on the gill covers and a golden colour with black stripes. I loved catching Perch but the lock keeper would eventually see us and we would have to move to the lock wall. It was still a good place to fish for Roach and Gudgeon. The lock keeper's wife had a little shop that sold sweets and pop, so we could spend a whole day there. When it was really warm we would swim in the shallows a little further up the river.

While I was living on Lincoln Road I made a couple of new friends, Kenny and Lol. These lads were into hunting and I soon found myself learning about ferrets, lurchers and long nets. Lol had an egg collection that was a far cry from my sawdust filled biscuit tins, and he had a polished wooden cabinet of draws that pulled out to display his eggs. He had chickens too and would hatch pheasant eggs using the broody chickens. Kenny had a fox cub as a pet for a while before he released it back into the wild. This was another side of nature and the countryside that I would embrace. It wasn't long before I was introduced to poaching. I loved going out on a moonless night with a lamp and a lurcher dog and catching a few rabbits or in the daytime finding a rabbit set, putting down purse nets, placing the ferret down the hole and waiting for the action. Nothing beats a good rabbit stew or pie and it was something we looked forward to. It was a new world to me and something I pursued for a lot of years. There was something about being out in the dead of night with a couple of dogs and a lamp that gave me a sense of peace and safety especially when I went on my own. It wasn't always so much about the hunting. For me, it was more about the solitude.

It seems that I am painting a dark picture and for me, at times, it was. There were also times when things were really good. My dad loved a drink and on a Sunday afternoon he might take Alan and me to the local pub with him where he would meet up with his friends for a drink. We would sit outside with a bottle of Vimto and a packet of Smith's crisps that had the salt in a twist of blue paper. In those days the pubs would close at two o'clock on a Sunday and we would walk back home for one of Mum's famous roasts with all the trimmings.

My dad was a keen fisherman and he was the one that taught me a lot about it. I have then been able to pass this on to my children and grandchildren. Fishing was such a valuable gift. I knew what it felt like to catch my first fish and now I could see that excitement not only in the faces of my children when they were little but now also in the faces of my grandchildren.

Sometimes there was a bus trip to Skegness and although those trips were more about the adults drinking all day, I somehow managed to find a way to fish in the dykes that ran down the side of the roads and catch small sea fish like Dabs, little flatfish. I was quite happy doing this and then the trip back on the bus with the obligatory stop at another pub halfway home.

I can only recall having one proper holiday and that was when our parents took us to Butlin's in Skegness. It was after Graham had died and so it was only Alan and I but we still had a whale of a time, left to our own devices while my mum and dad visited the bars. It was a kid's paradise, or that's how it felt at the time. We would wake up to the PA system blaring out someone singing about having a happy day and we would jump up all excited and head off to the restaurant for breakfast. Everyone was relaxed and happy and we would take off for the day after breakfast and join the queues for the rides. We would then meet up at mealtimes and be back to the chalet at night. That holiday was special. No arguing, no falling out. We were all just having fun and it didn't seem to matter that my mum and my dad spent it in the bars drinking most of the time.

The swimming pools were a big attraction to us and Butlin's had indoor and outdoor swimming pools. I had become quite a strong swimmer after plenty of practice in our local pool and the river, and one day they had a swimming competition at the holiday camp so I entered it. I can remember how nervous I was on the day. There were lots of spectators including my parents and it was a lovely warm summer day. The pool was looking good. We stepped up to the side of the pool and I was the smallest one there; the other kids were taller and some older. I am not sure if it was one or two laps but I know I wanted to make my dad proud of me for once. The starting gun went off and I dived in and swam my heart out. I could hear all this cheering and when it was over I had come second. I was so disappointed even though my dad told me most of the crowd were cheering me on to win and I got the biggest applause when I was given my award for a second. I remember thinking my dad and mum did seem proud, but I so wanted to win that race and prove something to my dad. It didn't happen and I was left disappointed. I didn't dwell on it too long and soon got back into the holiday spirit and off on a new adventure with my brother but that memory would still pop up now and again and the feeling of not quite being good enough was to be a constant companion.

# 4

## SHAME AND HUMILIATION

I don't think my mum could live with the
memories of that house on Lincoln Road. We
move out and into town to a house on
Appleton Gate. A lot of the roads in Newark
end with a 'gate' in the name. We have a castle
here and these roads signify the gates out of
the town when it had a wall around it

This next part of my story I am not over the
moon to write about and would maybe prefer
to leave it out but it is what I experienced and
so it is going to be written.

This was just after we moved into the new
house and, after school, my friends and I had
started sneaking into a Malt Kilns that was
only just around the corner from where I lived
and we would build dens among the sacks of

grain. There were hundreds of sacks on different floors and only one or two people were working there. They didn't seem to bother with us and so we would explore the different floors making our dens, we also found a covered-in disused bridge to another building on the opposite side of the road where all the heaps of malt were stored. The bridge was about thirty feet in the air. It was old. The wooden floorboards were old and rotting. It was dangerous to cross and so that made it more appealing to us.

We would spend hours there, and over after a while I got to know a worker called Alex. He would let me sit in a small room where he had his breaks and make me a cup of tea and he seemed ok and then he began to show me magazines with naked women in them. I was about thirteen by then. Sometimes I would sneak in on my own and explore or climb into a den and one evening when I had done this I bumped into Alex and he enticed me back to his tea room and began showing me the magazines with naked women in and then he started touching my private parts, and then he got me to do things to him sexually. I can remember feeling aroused and liking the feeling and then afterwards when it was over I was so ashamed and never dared to tell another soul about it. I held that secret for over thirty years. I was full of shame and it was not just about what he did to me but the thoughts that I might have liked it. This experience only added to my feelings that there was something wrong with me.

I was working on the local market helping the stallholders unload and set up their stalls before school and again after school, helping them load back up. I really enjoyed my days on the market. It was so vibrant with lots of customers. Wilf would bring freshly laid eggs and if he had cracked one he would show me how to put my head back and break it into my mouth and swallow it whole. I guess it was like a poor man's oyster but I did enjoy them. On Saturdays, I would work on the stall all day and earn some extra money. On one particular Saturday, I was working and must have gone around the front of the stall and there were quite a few people there and suddenly I could smell something that just sent this rush of fear through me and all the hairs on the back of my neck stood up. It was the distinctive smell of the Malt Kilns and then I saw him, he turned around and smiled and spoke to me. I was frozen in fear but worse still he had someone with him and he said something to him and they both smiled knowingly. I knew he had told him and I felt the shame and humiliation wash over me. I spent the rest of the day in shock but thankfully I never saw him again, ever!

I looked forward to my job on the market, they were lovely people. The market was always busy, all the stallholders knew each other and it was a real community. I worked for a few different stallholders. The market was on Wednesdays and Saturdays and I would work for Percy the Potman on Wednesdays and Wilf Bates or someone else on a Saturday. Unfortunately, I still had sticky fingers and would steal a few shillings to supplement my wages now and again. I wonder if stealing money was one of the reasons I was getting into trouble with my dad because I know I had taken money from my mum's purse occasionally to buy sweets.

I would spend a lot of any money I had on buying sweets. It was as if they made me feel better in some way. Something else that has just come to my mind... My mum had a pantry as most houses did at that time. It would have a stone or marble shelf to keep things cool. She would store cans of things in this pantry and build them up for Christmas or some other occasion and among these cans were large cans of fruit such as pears and peaches and because I had these cravings for sweet things, I would open the bottom of the can and drink all the sweet juice out and then eat the fruit. I would then wash it out, dry it and put it back in the pantry putting it at the bottom of the stack and hope to get away with it. It would come to light eventually but not for some time.

I was going to have two more run-ins with my dad in this house and that was going to be it. The first one was after he had started using his belt on me again. The belt is made of three coloured strips of leathers plaited together, red, green and yellow, and at the end is a bright brass buckle. This time when the beating started I had run outside to get away from him and was sitting on the fence at the end of the garden in just a pair of trousers and refused to come in. This was the first time I realised that they were worried about what the neighbours thought. We were living next door to a fish and chip shop and they would have their back door open and so now my mum and my dad were trying to coax me in with whispers and looking over their shoulders to see where the neighbours were. I eventually went in and was sent to bed but escaped any further punishment.

While writing this, I had a moment of clarity about a reason for part of my dad's rage. I spoke about how I had learned to find a way to somehow block out what he was doing to me, well along with that was a streak of defiance that was growing and I can remember that as I got older I refused to let him make me cry and then I started telling him that one day I was going to be big enough to hit him back. This would enrage him even more so and for some strange reason I felt as if I had some sort of power over him and this would encourage me to goad him because deep down I knew my day would come.

The second and last time didn't go so well, I might have pushed him too far. He had gone into one of his rages, and he was now using the buckle end of his belt as the other end had lost its effectiveness but things were about to go wrong. We were in the kitchen where this usually took place but in his temper, he had managed to hit the ceiling with the belt buckle and it had broken and now it had cut my back open quite deeply but he was so enraged I don't think he had even noticed. In the end my mum had to physically get between him and me to stop him carrying on. In a way, it was a blessing in disguise because that was the last time I can remember him beating me.

The thing is I don't know where my dad's uncontrollable rage came from; yes, of course, I wasn't helping the situation but it was his loss of any sort of control. He never talked about growing up or about his time in the army. I know he had two sisters that won a lot of money on the Irish lottery and then moved to Scarborough and lived in a big house with lots of cats. I met his mum and dad once or twice but that is all. I don't think they ever visited us. As to how he was brought up, I have no idea. He never spoke about it at all to me and so not only did I not know how he was treated as a child but I also had no knowledge of anything around him growing up.

The same goes for my mum. We met her mum once. She lived in Sandringham. I can remember walking around the grounds near the college with my cousin Susan. I just remember our grandmother dressed in black and when we were all in the room together on that one and an only trip we made, you could cut the atmosphere with a knife. It was obvious that something had gone wrong between them. There were no signs of affection, no hugs, it was cold and loveless but we were never told what the reason was and even in later years we never got to the bottom of it. Something that came to light when writing this which was shocking to both myself and my brother when I asked him about it, was that our mum had never mentioned at any time anything about her dad and we never saw him or even saw a photo of him. It was as if he never existed and I had never given him a thought until I was reading through this chapter and realised that he was missing and questioned why I had never thought of him before. It just adds to the mystery of why my mum was so distant from her mother. My mum's sister Celia, Susan's mum came over a couple of times but there were no real family ties and I didn't realise how distant they were until later in life. Even Susan, who we were in touch with after her mum passed, continued to stay in touch for a little while but then disappeared. Celia passed away some years ago and now we will step up our attempts to track down our cousin Susan, as she is the only remaining relative that may know the answer to the mystery.

Growing up in an environment of secrecy and not being able to talk about my feelings, not allowed to ask questions, being told that kids are to be seen and not heard and all the emotional and physical abuse, it is little wonder that it would be hard for me to build relationships. Even as a teenager I found it hard to talk to girls and could never approach someone I liked because of these overwhelming feelings of being inferior, ugly or stupid and the fear of being rejected and humiliated. I imagine all kids have a certain amount of these feelings growing up but mine seemed insurmountable. I found a way to overcome this when I was a little older but that comes later in the book.

I am coming to the end of my school days and it was about this time when me and my friends found a pub that would let us sit in the back room that they called the "snug" and as long as we were quiet and behaved ourselves the landlord would serve us beer. The pub was "The Generous Britain". It is long gone now but myself and two or three of my school mates would go in a couple of times a week and we thought it was great.

When it came to leaving school at fifteen with no qualifications I had already decided I wanted to be a welder and follow my dad into construction on the power stations, only because I knew this is where the big money was. In 1965 this wasn't a problem, anyone could pick up an apprenticeship and I went to a local company that built industrial boilers called Farrar's Boiler Works. I just went into the office and told them that I was about to leave school and wanted to be an apprentice welder and that was that. I was given a start date. It was a proud day for me because I had done it on my own and I had a chance to prove myself.

When I think back at how pleased my parents were and how I saw this as a turning point in my life, and how much different life was going to be, it was a time full of hope and it started well. I was there for about two and a half years and although the work was hard I enjoyed it. I was put with Bill Cranage, a lovely man that taught me about plating. This was marking the plates out before holes were punched in them and then it was rolled and made ready for the riveters. Yes, at that time they were mostly riveting the vessels but there were some welded ones. The apprenticeship included a day at college but despite my lack of any qualifications from school, I didn't struggle too much. I was also doing an evening welding school. I was working towards what I wanted to do and so I was making the effort and working hard.

Picking up my first wage packet was another proud day. I would get three pounds a week and I paid one pound board, a pound went in the bank and a pound for me. I still had my market job on a Saturday to give me a bit of extra money but eventually, that would go and I would work for Bill at the weekends. Bill had a chicken farm and one of the jobs was catching the chickens that were in an enormous barn. It was ok to start with, but catching the last few took a lot of doing and by the end of the day I was exhausted. I did love my job and the people I worked with, it felt as if I belonged to something at last but unfortunately it was going to be short-lived and I was about to be introduced to something that was going to eventually take over my life for the next thirty years!

# 5

## LIVING FOR THE WEEKEND

Was it my destiny or ill fate to grow up in the sixties? Whatever the reason I could never have envisioned where it would lead me.

At fifteen, I was making new friends and listening to the music of the time. Mostly The Beatles, but I also started listening to Motown music or Soul music; The Four Tops, The Temptations, Aretha Franklin and many more. There was a movement that went along with this music called Mods. Some of these Mods had scooters or Minis and dressed in certain clothes like Ben Sherman shirts, with stay press or two-tone trousers. We mostly wore faded denim jeans and jackets, and it had to be Levi's, Wrangler's or sometimes Lee Rider, although the Ben Sherman shirt was a must. We mostly went to local discos in those early days and we had a few in our area that we would often go to after work. Later, we would go to clubs but in the beginning it was just these small discos that would take place in church halls or community centres. They were all quite innocent and I don't remember any alcohol being around. Some of those that would show up were a bit older than me and already had scooters. The scooters were Lambrettas and Vespas with all the mirrors on and they all wore Parka coats that somehow seemed mandatory at that time if you owned a scooter. Often underneath these Parka coats, they would wear really smart suits with the Ben Sherman shirts, a tie and stylish shoes or desert boots, an ankle boot made of suede leather. There was also this other group of Mods that resembled skinheads; they were wearing denim and boots, but they weren't skinheads and it was these that I gravitated towards. It wasn't that we were two groups; we went to the same places and listened to the same music, we just dressed differently. It was Frank and Ronnie that first moved on to the minis. Frank had a minivan and Ronnie had a Mini Cooper car. They had both previously had scooters. After a while, some of the others decided to get minis too.

Music became a big part of this movement that had started in places like Brighton and filtered down to us in little old Newark. Although Motown and R&B music was the main music we followed, getting the latest

American releases and building a collection of our own was a big part of it too. In those early days, we had to go to Nottingham to find the rarer records, to a place called 'Selectadisc' in Arkwright Street. This was the place where you would find all the latest American imports and bootleg records (copies). It was a popular place not just for us but the black community as well, who were searching for the latest American "Blues" or "Reggae" music.

At that time Blues clubs were opening up in Nottingham like the AdLib, Beachcomber and Kool Kat Bar. This was mostly where the black guys went to listen to their music and had parties afterwards, usually at someone's house; these parties were also called "Blues". It wasn't long before we would start frequenting the clubs and parties to smoke cannabis with them, but here I go, getting ahead of myself. I am not sure when this all started but it wasn't long before we began using drugs and I was now about to be introduced to cannabis and amphetamines. It is not important which came first but what I do know is that I was hooked from the first time I ever took those amphetamines. It wasn't a physical addiction; it was how they made me feel. I don't think I could ever describe that feeling. It was as if everything that I worried about went in a puff of smoke. I wasn't thinking that there was something wrong with me, or that I was stupid, or different. I became super confident and suddenly found it easy to talk to girls and we were all in this together. It was a movement of working-class kids that worked in factories and offices during the week and lived for the music and the weekends. We looked out for each other and we started going out of town to soul nights and discos, travelling all over the place to anywhere that played our music. I never wanted it to end and this was going off all over the country! I felt part of this movement but more importantly, we were a tribe, a family, and I needed this. I needed to belong to something; this was a part of me that had been missing for a long time. I had always felt the outsider and now I didn't. I was home at last!

Our little band started to develop and some of those I remember were Frank- he was a good friend- and then there was Ronnie, Barry, Mitch, Terry, Henry, Bernard, John, to name a few. The girls were a big part of this movement too and had their own Mod clothes that included two-tone mini dresses and leather coats. I seem to remember a lot of black and white patterns. Pat, Isabel, Diane, Wendy and Kerry were mostly girlfriends of the boys in our little band. They all had scooters and would travel with the boys. I never owned a scooter or a minivan but it didn't seem to make much of a difference as there was always a spare place going in a car or van.

Sometime later, some of us started to travel off out of town to visit clubs and all-nighters. The all-nighters were to become known as Northern Soul all-nighters but in the beginning, it was Mods that were following DJs like Pete Stringfellow around the North. These all-nighters would start at 11pm on a Saturday night and finish at 7.30am on Sunday morning. The night would start by going to The Bowling Green (our local club) where the local DJ would be playing all the latest music, and then we would start taking our drugs. They took about an hour to start working. After that, we would leave the Bowling Green around 9pm and travel to the Twisted Wheel in Manchester, in the back of minivans and cars. This was one of the most famous venues for all-nighters in the country at the time. We had the customary Adidas bag with our change of clothes in and we'd head off over the Pennines to Manchester to dance through the night to the Soul and Motown music of the 60s. This is all I lived for at that time.

The Twisted Wheel was the first venue to hold all-nighters and would attract close to a thousand people. It also attracted the attention of the authorities who were well aware of the amount of drugs being taken as none of these types of club had an alcohol license. Not that anyone was interested in alcohol. Another unfortunate thing about the Twisted Wheel was that it was directly across the road from the Police Station. It was not unusual to have their drug squad come in and take a couple of people off the dance floor to be tested for drugs. After it was over we would be coming down off the drugs and starting to feel pretty rough. We would climb in the back of the minivan and make our way to Sheffield, to another club that I think was called the Fiesta Club. It opened early and quite a few people who had been at the all-nighter would meet there and we would have a few drinks before making the rest of the journey. When we got home it was usually to bed and try to get some sleep; we all worked and needed to be ready for Monday morning. We always managed to do it somehow, but very rarely bright-eyed or bushy-tailed. We worked for one reason and that was to do the same thing again the following weekend.

It was getting harder and harder to do for me to do all this on my apprentices' wages. Even though I had a raise, plus with the little extra I earned on the side, it wasn't enough. It wasn't long before the apprenticeship went and I joined some of my friends that were earning a lot more on a building site, so this was where I ended up much to the disappointment of my parents.

All the drugs at this time were from the result of a chemist break-in and were all in capsule form or tablets, with names like blueys, black bombers, green and clears, black and whites, etc. Everyone had their favourites. Bombers were the strongest and were made by a firm called Riker and so you would see quite a few t-shirts with "Riker Liker" on them. We knew people that were chemist breakers in Lincoln and we would travel on a Friday night to get our supplies and that's when the weekend started but they didn't always end up in Manchester. We began to go to other parts of the country like Bradford, a club there called The String of Beads, and other ones in Wakefield and Castleford whose names escape me. I think one was called the Chicken Shack. The Broken Wheel in Retford was a regular local weekend haunt for us and where they had all-dayers from 10am until 8pm and that's where I first saw Edwin Starr. Venues started bringing in the American stars that we were all following and we travelled all over the country to get a chance to see them.

Bank holidays were spent at the coast; our local one was Skegness and we would travel over in the minis and minivans, or some would come on scooters. We would take over the bars on the seafront, with names like The

Beachcomber. The highlight of these weekends were the regular run-ins with the bikers known as 'Greasers' to the Mods. These run-ins could involve two or three hundred people but I never saw anyone get any serious injuries, it was mostly just cut lips and black eyes and we usually came off on top. I saw it as a bit of fun and bravado. The bikers had their bar, which was called The Ship and was away from the front but within walking distance.

Drugs were always involved, as they were most weekends, but one particular weekend Pete Stringfellow was at a venue at the other end of the front and I am not sure if it was an all-nighter but it was an amazing night. Towards the end, Stringfellow came on the mic to say there was a load of Greasers outside looking for trouble and we all piled out and had a bit of a bust-up and then back to Stringfellow's music. Who would have known that he would become a world-famous multi-millionaire, a working lad from Sheffield's steelworks? The thing was, he knew what we wanted to hear and he was getting hold of music from America that no one else had heard of. As a result, he was building a massive following. This Mod subculture had grown from a working-class generation that was disillusioned with our parents' idea of life being about working for fifty years and dying, tied up with mortgages and paying things off on the drip! There had to be more to life than this and with a few pills, close friends and some amazing music we thought we had found it, even if it was for only two days a week!

The Who were really popular with the Mods and with titles like 'My Generation' and 'Won't Get Fooled Again' it's no wonder they were so popular.

I remember on one of these Mods and Rocker trips to Skegness I was arrested for fighting and held overnight at the local Police Station. On the way there the two policemen had threatened to just give me a good hiding and let me go and I tried to talk them into it because I didn't want my dad to find out but it never happened. After I had been locked up for a while an officer came down and said 'We have had to contact your dad because you are under eighteen and when we told him you were locked up he said "Good, keep him there"' I didn't expect anything different really but I was still left with a feeling of being cast out and alone. With everything I was doing I never once considered how my parents must have felt and it would be a long time before I would reach that point. The next morning was a Tuesday and I went before the magistrate and was fined or something for causing a disturbance and released but when I stepped out it was like a ghost town and I had no way of getting home, sixty miles away. Just after I came out of the court, a Hells Angel came out and when I asked him where he was from, he said Boston. It's funny that we were on opposite sides the day before and now here we were chatting away as if nothing had happened. Anyway, Boston was closer to home for me and you guessed it, I managed to get a lift off him and hitchhiked the rest of the way. I wasn't looking forward to going home to face the music and when I did things were a bit strained, to say the least. I was about seventeen and was thinking I was a bit of a Jack the Lad. Alan, my brother was around twelve and I can remember him being in the kitchen and he was posing in front of the mirror and I started taking the mickey out of him when he suddenly turned around and punched me and put me on my arse! He ran off with me in hot pursuit and ran through the front room, up the stairs and straight through my bedroom that had a window that lucky for him was open and he escaped onto a sloping roof and into the garden. I was fuming and when I went downstairs into the kitchen I found my mum in hysterics of laughter with tears streaming down her face and told me in no uncertain terms that I had it coming and deserved it and not to touch him. I must admit that once I had cooled down I did see the funny side of it.

My time at home was clearly coming to an end, though. One day there was an incident between my dad and I that I thought would make my day but it shocked me when it didn't.

# 6

# THE MOMENT I HAD WAITED FOR

It was a warm Saturday afternoon and I was at home when my mum and dad came staggering back from the local pub that was just up the road from us called The Newark Arms. I could see they were both quite drunk and I don't know what started it but Dad began shouting at me about being a waste of space and brought out his favourite saying: "You will never amount to anything as long as you have a hole in your arse!" I was in the front room as he said this and I just snapped and punched him on the jaw. At that, he went over a chair knocking the budgie's stand over and ended up being wedged behind the chair. My mum went into immediate action to save the budgie of all things. I stormed out.

This is the moment I thought I had been waiting for all those years. The times I had told him that one day this would happen and then when it did there were no feelings of triumph over him. I had played this scene out in my mind so many times and now it had come and all I felt was shame, guilt and a flood of emotions. I made my way to town with tears streaming down my face and unbelievable confusion about how I was feeling. This was supposed to be my "moment"; I had finally triumphed over this bully who it seemed had beaten me mercilessly at times for years. There was a part of me that felt cheated and another part of me that was wrestling with the thoughts that despite what he did, he was still my dad and he deserved more from me. I had always had it drilled into me that I should always respect my elders and seeing my dad in a heap on the floor didn't feel right. I went to a pub called The Cavalier, washed my face in the toilets and went drinking with my friends to try to drown out these confusing feelings.

It was my dad's birthday the next day and I bought him an electric shaver off the resident shoplifter; after all, it's the thought that counts! Anyway, another shock was on its way because my dad came looking for me and called me outside where I feared the worst. For the first and only time I can remember, my dad apologised to me and I also apologised to him and gave him his knocked off electric shaver to prove it!

I guess the saying "blood is thicker than water" must be true but I was getting closer to the time when I would need to leave home for good. I had run away from home before after violent arguments with my dad. This time I would end up in a caravan on Tolney Lane where our resident Romany community lived. There was something about the Romany people that I found quite appealing. I had been on my wanderings one day as a youngster and had come across a camp with the horse-drawn bow-top caravans and a campfire. I always remembered that when they noticed me curiously watching them they immediately invited me to sit with them around their fire and gave me something to eat and drink and how welcomed they made me feel. Those I came to know now lived in modern caravans and were mostly scrap dealers. They spoke Romany and come to that, so did I and a number of my friends because there were so many in our town. We soon got to know them and picked up the language.

There were no real amenities on the site I was on, besides a toilet block. When I needed to I would use the local council-run Public Baths known as "slipper baths" where I could get a hot bath and towels for a few pence. I also had friends and families that put me up for the odd night but this was going to be a bit more serious and was going to be for quite a long time. I had decided I wasn't going back, EVER! After a few weeks, I changed my mind. I couldn't live like this. I felt like a tramp and this wasn't in keeping with the clean cut Mod image that I was trying to portray and not only that I had never paid bills before such as rent, gas and electricity. It was taking a big chunk out of what money I had. I knew I had to bite the bullet, swallow my pride and get home somehow.

One day I went to see my mum after she finished work and told her where I had been living. She was appalled and I was soon back home. I promised not to cause any problems. I bit my lip and didn't argue; I needed to get back in the house. My dad was still working away from home so I only had to keep out of his way at the weekends and that wasn't too hard to do but I was on the verge of really messing this arrangement up.

The Bowling Green, our local club was gaining more popularity and people were travelling from other towns around us, like Nottingham, Lincoln, Worksop and Mansfield to hear and dance to the latest Motown and R&B music. We got to know some girls that travelled on the train to these nights out and sometimes I would take my dad's car from the lockup where he kept it while he was working away from home and drive them back to Retford or Worksop.

I had only been allowed back home a few weeks earlier when I started to sneak the keys out of the house, go to where it was housed, open the garage doors and first check where the petrol gauge was, so I could be sure that when I put it back there was about the same amount of petrol in the tank and I wouldn't get caught out. At that time I am sure I was not old enough to drive and so I don't think I even had a provisional licence.

On one of these jaunts to take these girls home to Retford, I lost control of the car and it went into a field, turned over a couple of times and was written off. Luckily nobody was seriously hurt. I had a cracked collarbone. There were four of us in the car; Sue, who was my girlfriend at the time, her friend, me, and my mate Tony. When it was all over with the police, ambulance and the hospital, a police officer handed me a tax disc and this was all that was left of my dad's car! It was scrapped!!

I went straight home, packed a bag, put the tax disc on the kitchen table, told my mum briefly what had happened and announced that I was leaving before my dad got home! I could see the shock on her face but I never waited for a response. It was late; Alan was asleep in bed. I left the house with a bag of clothes and no real idea where I would go. I was barely seventeen.

Figure 3 - Mum and Dad

My next temporary home was on the outskirts of Worksop, in a mining village called Manton. The pit was on the edge of the village and I was staying with a relative of a friend of mine, Malk Walker. Malk didn't warn me but also staying at the house was a young boy of about fourteen years and he had these terrible injuries after playing on the slag heap next to the colliery. From what I understood, sometimes this waste from the mines (coal dust) caught fire below ground, some sort of spontaneous combustion creating pockets of burning coal dust below the surface of the slag heap. I suppose like me these kids had been warned about the dangers and ignored them and while young Joe was playing he had fallen through into one of those burning pockets. The resulting injuries were terrible and I only saw his hands and face. His hands were badly scared and I seem to remember a couple of fingers missing but although I never saw the rest of his body, his face was in a terrible state and quite horrific; it was hard not to look away. Joe had no ears and no nose, just holes and lots of other disfigurements that I don't need to elaborate on, but as horrific as it was, it was also surprising how quickly I got used to it. I can remember talking to him and forcing myself to look straight at him because I can only imagine what it must have been like to have people turning away or making comments. I am not sure how long I stayed at that house. Maybe a month or so.

I needed to work and soon found a job. I had friends in Worksop and we would still be using amphetamines on the weekends. I had a few different jobs while I was there. When I was working as a window cleaner there, the boss made the mistake of talking to me like my dad and suffered the consequences. I also worked in a wood mill using a massive circular saw bed to cut tree trunks up to make pallets, but the one that stuck in my mind was in a foundry. It was like a scene from Dante's

Inferno. It was hot and dirty and work was brutal but the money was good so I stuck it out for a while.

I was with Susan by this time, who was to become my first wife. After meeting her at The Bowling Green when I was still living in Newark, she had been in my dad's car the night when I had the accident. I don't remember much about those early days other than drinking and taking drugs with her and my friends (who were also her friends that she had known before we met up). She was the real reason I ended up in Worksop at that time.

Susan's parents ran a public house called The Anchor in Worksop and I would spend time there in those early days. One day, I learned they were moving to another public house in a place called Markham Moor, which was about ten miles from Worksop on the edge of the A1. At this time I was staying with them but it meant I had to hitchhike to work every day in Worksop. I don't know how long I kept this up for.

Anyway, the long and the short of it was that Susan fell pregnant and eventually I decided I needed to go back to Newark with her and tell my parents. Well, that was it! As soon as I told my mum that Sue was pregnant, she took over! We were getting married. There were no ifs or buts about it; you have to do the right thing. We were told we couldn't have a child out of wedlock because of my mum's Catholic beliefs. I was nineteen and Susan was eighteen and I wouldn't dream of questioning my mum; this wasn't up for debate and so the date was set.

After the wedding at the Catholic church, we moved in with my mum and dad again and I was back in my old bedroom. I didn't relish the thought of being back at home again and it didn't feel comfortable. Our son, Steven was born while I was still at my parents and it wasn't long after this that we found our own place. I don't think my mum and Susan got on so I think it was a relief for all concerned when we moved out. Just before Steven was born I had started working with my dad on the power stations. We went to a station that was being built in Warrington in Lancashire called 'Fiddlers Ferry'. I absolutely loved it. I was living in billets, which consisted of several big wooden buildings with a corridor and rooms on either side. In each room was heating, two beds and a couple of wardrobes. Showers and sinks were a communal affair. We were charged so much a week, which included breakfast in the canteen.

There must have been a thousand men on that site and quite a few lived in the billets. This was my introduction to contract work. I had learned how to weld and to start with I was put in the workshop and allowed to practice. I was introduced to the shop steward and joined the mandatory trade union. I was then a card holding member of the Constructional and Engineering Union (CEU) constructional section. I stayed a member for 50 years.

I eventually went on to the main site into this massive building with all the noise and cranes, winches lifting steel, the welding and grinding and so many people. I was both scared and excited at the same time. The building was 200 feet high.

I took to this life like a duck to water. I was newly married and earning more money than I could have dreamed of. I loved the camaraderie working in a tough industry with these men that were rough and ready but looked out for each other. I was the youngest there at the time and they paid me special attention. I guess I felt special for the first time in a long time.

I worked hard and it took a little time to get used to. One of the things that started off being a shock to the system and then became just something that was inevitable was people quite often falling from heights and being killed. I never heard of anyone falling and being injured before; it seemed to be always instant death. Whenever this happened the whole site would have the following day off as a show of respect and then they would organise a collection for the family and everyone would be expected to contribute with no exceptions.

Something else that I found exciting about the job was overcoming the fear of heights and then the buzz of being out on open steel hundreds of feet in the air and knowing that one wrong move would mean certain death. I loved this feeling; I was a risk-taker and that would become apparent in so many other areas of my life. I later learned that there is a fine line between fear and excitement and I would constantly seek out ways to test my theory.

I was paired up with a plater (fabricator). His name was Pete and he was from Pontefract. He was a lovely man who didn't mind showing me the ropes. I wasn't confident in my welding abilities but to be fair I am sure I was doing ok. Part of our job was to fix the outer skin (sheet metal) to the outside of this enormous boiler. It entailed welding short scaffold tubes to the steelwork but you would only weld the top half of the tube so they could be easily broken off when it was time to move. These half-welded tubes would have two scaffold boards thrown on them and that was the platform for Pete and me to work on and Pete weighed about eighteen stone! To start with my heart would be in my mouth every time we climbed on. One bank holiday weekend when I was at home, Pete fell and was killed. I always remember being horrified when I was put back on the exact job he had been doing; when I got there one of his shoes was still on the floor and there were bloodstains on the wall. I reluctantly went to start work but fortunately my supervisor, a man called Ben Bassett heard about it and came up to me and moved me to a different job. I heard later that he was livid and had a right go at whoever put me back on that job.

There are so many stories I could tell you about that job but it would take up too many chapters of this book but I will tell a couple more...

We all were paid in cash on a Thursday at the end of the shift and some of the lads would go to the local casino every Thursday night and I got them to start taking me but the rule was that I would hand over my wages. They would allow me so much and then they would give me the rest back the next morning. They were all from Newark and knew my dad and also knew that I hadn't been married long and had a baby on the way. They made sure I didn't lose it all on the roulette wheel.

I can't remember my dad ever going to the casino. Most nights I would find him in the site bar playing cards with his mates. He wasn't the adventurous type and I think he liked to keep a low profile. I started to notice something else about him; he didn't stand up for himself and never got into confrontations even if someone was disrespectful to him. I was not like him and if anyone took a liberty with me I would address it and I did need to on a couple of occasions while I was there. They were lads about my age and just testing me. I was not following in Dad's footsteps regarding keeping a low profile and eventually I started getting some attention from the young canteen girls and had a couple of flings with them while I was there. I think that my dad was far from happy about it but I can't remember him ever said anything to me about it.

We all got in the cars for the journey home to Newark on a Friday afternoon and there would be about fifteen or twenty of us. The journey was over 'Snake Pass' and the roads were quite treacherous at times. On one particular journey we came across a pretty serious accident where we saw one car that was on its side with the wheels still spinning, so we knew it had only just happened. We all got out to see if we could help and Peter (one of our lot) ran up to the car and shouted, "Are you ok?" The driver replied, "Yes, fine", with which Peter responded "You fucking lucky bastard!" No sooner had he said it but a head popped up through the open window and it was a vicar! Well, we were mortified but the vicar just took it in his stride and smiled. We had a good laugh on the way home.

Another accident we had one night on the way home was this... It was just my dad and myself travelling in terrible conditions. It was snowing hard and we were going up a long steep hill when a car coming in the opposite direction decided to overtake the car in front of him and after he realised he wasn't going to make it he braked and skidded into us. We crashed. The radiator was broken and so we were stranded but the other car was just dented. We moved our car onto the side of the road to be picked up and then the other driver was about to leave and my dad said nothing. I was livid and let the driver know in no uncertain terms that he would be taking us to a train station so that we could get home seeing that it was his fault we were stranded. He agreed but I realised something then about my dad that I had suspected from seeing him at work and that was this: Dad was a coward when it came to standing up to someone his own size.

It was about this time that my son, Steven was born. It must have been on a weekend because I can remember going out to celebrate with a couple of mates Alan Salmon

(Sam) and Lush Warriner. I got so drunk that night that my mum and her friend had to put me to bed. I had been drinking whisky and for years afterwards the very smell of whisky made me nauseous. I was so happy and proud to have a son but regrettably, I was to fail him as a father.

My whole experience of that Fiddlers Ferry job was a bit crazy but I loved it. The shop steward for the site was a full Cherokee Indian and at some point he was sacked for clocking in somebody else. Then one day he turns up in full regalia, a Chief's headgear including a tomahawk and doing a war dance outside the main office. Well, you can imagine the whole scene and most of the site came to a standstill as more and more people came to see this spectacle. He even brought a couple of squaws with him, who also joined in the dancing.

I never worked on the same job with my dad as he was a different trade to me but I would sometimes go to where he was working. He was fitting the banks of boiler tubes that formed the wall of the boiler and by this time I had got my head for heights and would climb up the steelwork to where he was. I felt a sense of pride as I climbed up to where he was as he looked down watching my progress. I am sure he was proud of me too but he would never say it. One day I would get a chance to work on a power station with one of my sons but I am getting ahead of myself, again.

It was on this site where I first saw a scaffolder building a hanging scaffold by attaching a scaffold tube to the steelwork in the roof and slide down that tube that had a clip attached to stand on and start building out from that point with nothing but fresh air below them for two hundred feet. It was scary just watching and knowing that one mistake would be fatal. I guess they were adrenaline junkies and I now knew what that felt like.

I was there for just over a year and eventually it came to an end. I never worked with my dad again although I did return to power station work a few years later.

# 7

# CROWN COURT

After I was made redundant from the power station, I was still living at my parents' house with my wife and son but it wasn't working out. At some point, we found an upstairs flat on a street called Winchelsea Avenue in the town and moved in. It was the first time either of us had had our own place and we began to decorate and furnish it and made it our own. Steven was only a few months old and I hoped that we might make things work out even though the marriage was a bit shaky, to say the least, but it wasn't to be and deteriorated quite quickly when after a few months I went back to using drugs again.

I had been working as a welder in the early part of our life at the flat. I had no transport at that time and would cycle about 6 miles to

Southwell every weekday to a small fabrication shop. We built hydraulic, telescopic arms that fitted on the back of lorries and pumped concrete into multi-story buildings. Eventually one of the workers, a Polish guy that travelled from Newark in his Reliant Robin would give me a lift in exchange for a box of Hamlet cigars once a week. I enjoyed that job, it was a small family run business, owned by this big gentle man with a booming voice called Ackerman. The building was an old mill with a stream outside called 'The Greet'. It was a private trout fishing stretch of the stream but I would bring just a fishing reel in my lunch bag to work. In my breaks, I would sometimes sit on the grassy bank and free line a piece of bread down this brook and catch the odd trout; they loved my salmon and shrimp paste sandwiches.    I watched the bread bobbing along the surface of the water until a nice fat rainbow trout came up and took my bait. I can still see the colours flash in the shallow clear stream as the sun caught its flanks as it struggled to escape. This was my tea when I arrived home

My love of fishing would always stay with me and I soon had a fine collection of fishing tackle and was taking part in local fishing matches or just fishing for pleasure. I found this pastime gave me a sense of peace. It took me back to a time and place where I felt safe and life was good. Sat in the sun with my brothers, bright blue skies, a shimmering river, lots of fish to catch and we were all so happy. In that moment, life was perfect. I think I spent the rest of my life trying to recapture those moments.

I was trying to live a normal, married life but I couldn't settle and never felt content. I always felt as if I was missing out. Most of my friends were still living the single life. I was torn between wanting my freedom and the responsibility of bringing a child into the world. I felt trapped and the marriage was beginning to suffer. I didn't realise it at the time but I was desperate to be loved and would attach myself to any female at that time that showed me the slightest attention. I desperately wanted a loving relationship but had no idea what a loving relationship was. Sue and I had been together about six months before she became pregnant and this was the longest relationship I had been in and here we are married with a child!

Things were about to go downhill really quickly after I started to visit Lincoln again and it wasn't long before I am using amphetamines. To begin with it was only occasionally, but it always started this way and it would always end up escalating out of control. Somehow I would try and fool myself into believing it would be different this time but it never was. As soon as I took that first drug it became like a snowball rolling down a mountainside picking up speed and getting bigger until it hit something and smashed.

My next mistake was to become friendly with a little gang that had been breaking into chemists and were known as the main chemist breakers in the Lincoln area at the time. They always had money and drugs and after a while I grew tired of paying for my drugs and made a decision to start getting my own. It wasn't long before I had broken into my first chemist. It wasn't hard in those days (1970) and my way in was usually through an upstairs window, or through the roof by climbing a drainpipe. I always felt somewhat safe once I had reached the roof. There was much less security in those days, no police helicopters and when I reached an upstairs window it was usually a sash window that was easily opened. My head for heights was now being used for an altogether different reason.

I was hooked in more ways than one. I loved

the adrenalin rush of breaking into these places and the feeling the drugs gave me. I was doing this on my own and managed to avoid the attention of the police for some time. It wasn't too long before all that changed and I hooked up with a guy from Newark called Mick Fryer (Frizzel) and then after a while the three chemist breakers from Lincoln: Tom, Steve and Tam.

Once I had joined up with these guys, things were going to spiral out of control and would take a turn for the worse really quickly. By early 1971 I had regular unmarked police cars outside on the street watching my flat. We thought it highly amusing after a night out to creep up behind the car and bang on the roof and make them jump out of their skins. We always believed we were smarter than them and it became a cat and mouse game that I never took seriously. We were now having to travel further afield to take the heat off us a bit. Whenever we got back after a job we would strip off and put all our outer clothes in the washing machine our trainers would go in a bag and get disposed of, we would only keep a small amount of drugs in the house for personal use and if we got raided they would be flushed straight down the toilet. This became my way of life. It became a game of always trying to keep one step ahead of the police.

Sometimes I would go out on a Friday night and not come back until three days later when I had to face the music. I had some strange idea that coming back with a pocket full of money after selling a proportion of the drugs I had stolen over the weekend- and giving the cash to my wife- would make everything alright. After all, I would go away for a week when I was working with my dad. But this was just wishful thinking. My grasp on reality was slipping away. I wanted to believe that what I was doing only affected me and I stopped considering my family and justified it by providing money.

I was in this dilemma where I didn't want to be married and I questioned if I had ever been in love with Susan. I felt I had been railroaded into this marriage by my mum because of the pregnancy but now at the same time I couldn't bear the thought of my son Steven calling someone else "Daddy". This thought would sometimes consume me and fill me with anger. I knew I would lose them one day but I had no idea how painful that was going to be for all concerned.

The police raids became more frequent and

often the front door would be forced open and the police would pile in and turn the flat upside down searching for drugs. Very rarely would they find any in the house. I was very careful.

We thought we were too smart for the police but our little house of cards was about to come crashing down. I had bought a car from one of the Lincoln crew's girlfriends. The car was bought with drugs and no cash changed hands. Now we had a car of our own, the matter of none of us having a licence didn't seem to come into the equation!

We called it our 'getaway car' but it was an old late 1950s Ford Anglia. On one occasion after a break-in with Frizzel, we were making our way back to this so-called getaway car with the proceeds. It was parked in the corner of a public car park. We put everything in the car jumped in and proceeded to start it, ready for our speedy escape but the battery was flat so we resorted to pushing it up and down the carpark at three o'clock in the morning trying to bump start it   and instead of any concerns that we might be caught we were both in fits of laughter over the absurdity of it all. We did get away but it was far from the speedy escape we envisioned.

We were still only using amphetamines but what was happening was that we were also accumulating a large number of hard drugs that we kept hidden in a suitcase. In this suitcase were ampoules of injectable heroin, cocaine, morphine etc. and we had a plan to go to London and sell them and make a fortune. We had no contacts and no idea how much they were worth but on the other hand, we knew if we got caught with them we would be doing some serious prison time. So, because we were now getting so much police attention we decided to get rid of them and the suitcase was duly dispatched off a bridge into our local river. I would often fantasise that the next time they drained that part of the river I would go and find this suitcase and make a fortune from the proceeds.

A memory that comes back to haunt me every now and again is of being at Mick's house in Balderton, which is a part of Newark. His house wasn't as well known as my flat and we were there using drugs and fooling about with a couple of girls. I can't remember who they were but I kept a folding 410 shotgun at his house that I used when I went out poaching. This shotgun was a double barrel and had a hammer mechanism that meant you would physically pull the hammers back until they locked in place and then use the trigger to fire it. On this gun, one of the hammers didn't work but it was still possible to pull the hammer back and release it and it would still fire the cartridge. I had been fooling about with this girl pulling the hammer back and pretending to shoot her at close range. Anyway, I stopped and went to put the gun away and when I opened the gun there was a live cartridge in the chamber with the defective hammer! I instantly went into a cold sweat at the thought of what could have just happened! It still to this day sends a shiver down my back.

I was married in 1970 and it was now 1972 my marriage was coming to an end and I was about to have my first experience of being in front of a Judge at a Crown Court. It all started with a plan to go to Retford where we had found two chemists that seemed pretty easy, so off we went and decided to split up and do one each. Frizzel and I would do one, Tom and Steve would do the other. Our driver Tony would stay in the car hidden in a back street and off we went. We did our job and made our way back to the car but when we got there a police car was parked next to it and our driver was being questioned.

We split up and headed off in different directions. It was the early hours of the morning and I decided to make my way back home cross country. It was just over twenty miles and I was completely paranoid. I had a bag of drugs from the chemist that I was dipping into. I was so scared and thought if I can just get home I will be safe. I had always felt that I had a certain amount of control over the outcomes at home. I didn't leave evidence, I controlled the amount of drugs in the house and didn't have a problem being questioned because I always felt I had covered everything but now I had no idea what would happen. When I got to within a couple of miles from home it was getting light and so I saw a bus to Newark at a terminal in a village called Tuxford, so I boarded it and arrived in Newark where I hid the drugs in a derelict house and took a taxi home. I walked in the house thinking, at last, I was safe only to be told by Susan that the police had already been there looking for me.

Now the chase was on. I had outrun a couple of detectives across a local park and managed to hide in the boiler room of a Territorial Army building. I remember it being a coal boiler; warm and dark. I curled up next to its warmth for a little comfort but feeling like a trapped animal. I decided to stay there until it got dark and retrieve the drugs I had hidden and get to some friends in another town but that plan soon went out of the window when the janitor came in to stoke the boiler and I made a bolt for it.

I was so determined not to be caught and the chase went on for another hour before they finally caught me when I tried to outrun a police dog across a farmer's field on the outskirts of town. From here I was taken to Newark police station and questioned. I had injuries from the dog encounter and was taken to the hospital in handcuffs to be treated and then returned to Newark police to be transported to Retford police station. At this point, I had not slept for more than forty-eight hours and was not being very cooperative, to say the least.

The next morning I would be made to do my walk of shame!! I was being walked from the Retford police station to the magistrate's court, which were a few buildings away from each other. I had torn clothes and some red antiseptic from the hospital on my wounds, my trainers had been sent to forensics and I had been given a pair of wellingtons, so you can imagine how I looked. I was so embarrassed and humiliated as they walked me to the court past shoppers on the street staring at me and their children pointing at me as their mums pulled them away.

The court appearance was short and we were all remanded into Lincoln prison where we would remain until sentence about two or three months later. When that eventually happened on the tenth of April 1972, I received two years imprisonment suspended for twelve months. I was so relieved that I wasn't going back to prison but my relief was to be short lived.

That evening I was at the local club celebrating my good fortune when a friend of mine pulled me to one side to tell me one of my other friends- John- had been having an affair with my wife Susan while I had been locked up. I was full of rage. John was at the club with some people I didn't know but that wasn't going to stop me. I asked a couple of mates to watch my back and went to find him but he must have spotted me and he was gone. I spent all night searching for him. I went to his house a couple of times asking his pregnant wife where he was. The next morning he had come home and I went into his room and attacked him and didn't stop until I was exhausted. This was the start of a vendetta that went on for some time, every time I saw him no matter where it was I would attack him again.

I was so enraged and felt so betrayed and hurt so deeply by what they had done especially as Susan was pregnant at the time and so that brought up a whole new set of suspicions-"How long has this been going on and is the child mine?" I was a mess and I was so angry and all this anger was directed at John. John had been a good friend and he came from a large Irish Catholic family of mostly boys. I was obsessed with making him pay for what he had done but all through this I never once questioned my behaviour. I never looked at how I was missing a lot of the time that my drug-using friends were at the house, a lot of people were turning up to do business from other cities, that our house was often under surveillance and that we were getting raided. In my crazy, drug-fuelled thinking I thought as long as I was putting money on the table none of this mattered and I seemed to also totally disregard my own philandering and disappearing for days on end. How must Susan have felt? It was all about what she and John had done to me and it would be a long time before I looked at what I was doing and my own part in all this. Tom, who was one of our little crew, said to me that at the end of the day the man can make his advances to a woman as often as he likes but in the end it's the woman that has to agree. This somehow made sense to my drug-addled mind.

I had one last fight with John outside one of our local pubs called The Rutland Arms on a Wednesday afternoon, I remember what day it was because it was a market day and there were a lot of shoppers about but that hadn't stopped me attacking him. When we had finished I said to him, "John, this has gone on long enough" and he agreed, we shook hands and went into the pub and I bought him a pint. It was over.

A few days later I was in prison and heard that John had died. He had a rare disease that can cause the main artery (aorta) to rupture and overexertion can be a factor or so I was told. I hoped our fights over the previous weeks hadn't contributed to it. I was told he had been riding his bike when it happened but it still played on my mind and despite everything, I was going to miss him, he was my friend, and I was so pleased that we had made our peace on that last time that I saw him

I don't think at this time I really understood, let alone admitted how out of control my life had become. I thought I could firefight and juggle at the same time. I was trying to control my situation and everyone involved in my little enterprise and thought I had all my bases covered. I was about to have a rude awakening that would bring my little house of cards tumbling down!

# 8
## NO WAY OUT OF THIS

My life was now officially a 'car wreck'. I had gone completely off the rails over the previous few weeks. To be truthful, I had been off the rails for quite some time but this was really bad! The police had stopped one of our accomplices in his car and when they searched it they found all the empty bottles from the chemists that we had broken into. He was supposed to have thrown them in the river on his way home but for some reason, he hadn't. When the bottles came back from the forensic team our fingerprints were all over them. I am not sure how many chemists the others were involved with but I ended up being charged with breaking into fourteen chemists, just thirteen days after getting a suspended sentence for the same thing! My marriage was all but over, my friend was dead and I didn't know if I was ever going to see my son again.

The main thing I can remember is all my anger was with other people: "If they hadn't have done this, that, or the other then I wouldn't be in this predicament". I was in total denial lockdown! I didn't know it at the time but this is a trait that would stay with me for most of my life. I would refuse to take responsibility for the consequences of my actions. It had to be somebody else's fault but here I was again being processed through the prison system and taken to my cell.

I remember that first morning. I was laid in bed and I could feel the warm sun on my face as it came through the window, I stretched and opened my eyes and then a feeling of utter dread came over me as the realisation dawned on me of where I was and what I was facing. Up until now I hadn't had a prison sentence as such, I had only experienced being on remand where you were allowed to wear your own clothes, have meals brought in, and have visits every day and sure enough I was on remand again but now a prison sentence was inevitable. There was no way out of this!

I am not sure if Susan came to visit me or if I saw Steven again at this point. I didn't want to see her but I missed my son. Susan had been working at Balderton Hospital, a secure unit in Newark when all this came to light about the affair. I went to the hospital to confront her about it and was told to leave by the staff and eventually the police were called to remove me. From what I remember, Susan stayed at the unit to keep out of my way and I wouldn't see either of them again for quite some time.

I knew I was going to be on remand for two or three months so I had to just get on with it. My co-accused were there so we would try to pair up and get a cell together. The cells consisted of a single bed, a bunk bed, a table, a chair and a bucket to piss in. We would get three meals a day and exercise where we would walk around the main yard in circles for an hour. We also had a chance to use the gym every morning after breakfast and I looked forward to this. They had a gym officer that would set up a circuit. It was brutal and quite often I would lose my breakfast in the loo but it just felt as if I was doing something useful.

Well, the day of reckoning finally arrived and it was 'Crown Court Day'. There were four of us: me, Mick, Tom, and Steve. Tam had left the crew by this time; he must have been smart enough to see where it was all going and bailed out on us. We stood in front of the judge as the charges were read out and at some point he questioned my charges of thirteen chemist burglaries so shortly after my last sentence and he was assured it was accurate. At this point, I was seriously bricking it; this was going to be my first prison sentence and I was fearing the worst.

So, it comes to sentencing: we all stand up and the judge deals with my accomplices first. One by one they are sentenced to two years imprisonment and taken away. I am shaking in my boots as to what he has in store for me but to my utter surprise, I am given a two year probation but with it was a condition of residence at a drug treatment facility in the city.

This could have been a turning point in my life but did I take advantage of it? Not a chance!! I just saw it as a result, an opportunity to screw the system and I just had to find a way to get out of there as soon as possible. The court order said that they couldn't keep me for more than a year but I had no intentions of staying that long.

I was taken to a place called Porchester House in Nottingham and taken for assessment. I had been on remand for almost three months so I had no drugs in my system but they insisted on medicating me. One of the drugs they administered was Largactil, which among other things is an antipsychotic drug also known as the 'liquid cosh'. I found myself walking around like a zombie for much of the time.

I was in no way compliant with the treatment or with what was being asked of me but at the same time I couldn't afford to be thrown out and back to the courts, so I had to be careful how far I went. Most of the patients there were either alcoholics or injecting heroin addicts. I didn't like these people and certainly wasn't like them. I only used amphetamines. I would refer to them as 'dirty junkies' and 'low life drunks'. I wasn't making many friends but when I realised that I was not going to get out of there any time soon I started to settle down and 'play the game'.

The resident psychiatrist was a man called Dr. Williams and he was a nice enough man and would patiently listen to my ramblings but one day he said something to me after I had been explaining to him why I wasn't like any of his other patients. He said, "One day you will be back here or somewhere like this place and you will be just like one of them. You will be an injecting heroin addict or an alcoholic." I can remember laughing at him and saying "You must be joking, that will never happen" but he could obviously see something in me that I couldn't see for myself. Not only was he right but it wasn't even going to be that far away.

While I was there, I had met a young lad. I am not sure how old he was at that time but he had been one of the youngest heroin addicts in the country after being introduced to it at fourteen by his elder brother. His name was Kevin and we would spend quite a bit of time listening to music, although I wasn't too keen on his taste of Velvet Underground and Neil Young.

I think at this point my wife Sue had started coming to visit me there and I think we were trying to patch things up. I was more interested in my son Steven than her, even though I knew that I had let him down badly. Now there was another baby on the way that I wasn't even sure was mine. It was a mess but every now and again I would be allowed out for a day and sometimes a weekend. We would hire a car and drive about or go to the coast. I think at this time the flat had gone and she was staying with her parents. I got a chance to spend some time with my son but that was about it. I couldn't forget what had happened, as much as I tried. I had a picture in my head of Sue and John together that wouldn't go away and brought up a multitude of feelings; these feelings of inadequacy and not being good enough that would leave me with a ball of anger and frustration in the pit of my stomach.

Anger and rage became my constant companions. I was trying to settle into this rehab way of life because I knew it was Dr. Williams's decision when I could leave and I would need to toe the line, so to speak. I don't know how often this happened but now and again they had what the residents named the

'Nutter's Ball'. Porchester House had two main buildings. One was the rehab facility and the other bigger building housed the patients with mental health problems and when they had this Ball (which was a disco really) they put us all together. I can't remember much about it other than meeting this old guy that was convinced he was Admiral Nelson. After I first met him, I would often see him walking in the gardens and always make a point of greeting him with his rightful title of "Admiral".

The gardens were well looked after and had winding paths through them that I often spent time walking on an evening. We were taken on trips out now and again and one of these trips was to a Monastery just outside Newark called Kelham Hall where we were able to meet the monks and walk around the beautiful grounds. It's quite ironic because I live next to Kelham Hall now and have done for a number of years and have spent a lot of time in the grounds and fishing in the river at the back of it, although the monks have long gone.

Another trip that stayed with me was the trips to a special needs school that we would visit quite often. We would buddy up with one or two of these kids who had different problems or some form of autism. When I first went to the school, I was a bit apprehensive that these kids would just come straight up and start touching us and feeling our hair and I didn't know what to do. Eventually, I realised that they were extremely affectionate and loving and some just wanted to be hugged and to hug me and lay their head on my chest. I started to really look forward to those days and seeing their happy faces when we came through the door. While I was there, I noticed a pretty little girl around six years old that seemed healthy in every way and I asked about her and was told that she hasn't been given a diagnosis. She has nothing wrong with her but there is nowhere else for her to go. I found that so sad and I often wondered what happened to her.

It was coming to the end of my stay at Porchester House and while I had been there I had met a lady from Ollerton, a small mining village about eight miles outside Newark who offered me a flat above a shop she owned there. I moved in with Sue and Steven. He must have been about three by now. The flat was a pokey little hole but it was a start. I can't remember if Jane had been born by then but if not it must have been close. This was a rough mining village but I seemed to get on with the locals alright. Sunday morning would see them down on the local playing field Whippet racing and playing pitch and toss. That being a game where the players toss a coin towards a mark. The one that is closest to the mark then tosses all the coins in the air and he gets all the ones that land on heads; all the remainder are left for the next game. I liked my Sunday mornings with this mining community.

Things were not working out at home and although I had wanted to give it a go for the sake of the children, I couldn't do it. We would just argue all the time and we were both miserable. I had started meeting up with Kevin, the young lad I had met in rehab and it wasn't long before I was using drugs again. Whenever I found myself struggling with painful feelings, I would always turn to drugs and try to medicate my way out of them. I carried on using with Kevin for a little while and then one night I made a fateful decision. I decided to break into a chemist in the local village, taking into consideration that the police station was a couple of hundred yards from where our flat was and the chemist was on the road at the back of us. It was a suicide mission, but I went anyway. I went in through the roof and took the drugs and got home but what happened next has always baffled me. I was always so careful not to leave any evidence and this time was no different but I fully expected the police to be at my door the next morning or to be arrested at some point. I was still on probation after the rehab so they would know where I was living.

When I did eventually get arrested I was quietly confident that I would walk out of there but what I didn't know is when I was climbing into the roof I had dropped my UB40 (dole card) with all my details on it!!

I had these delusions of being too smart for the police and I could always stay one step in front of them but the evidence told a different story. I was about to have my third appearance in front of a judge in a crown court in less than a year and this time it was a prison sentence for sure.

What bothered me the most was that I had nobody to blame. How could I do something so stupid? I even wondered if I had somehow done it on purpose to escape my situation of being with someone I didn't trust or love and at the same time knowing that my children needed a father. I didn't want to abandon them. Even the baby she was carrying that I wasn't sure was mine still needed to have a father. This mess wasn't the children's fault. I knew I had let them down badly and I had wanted to leave Susan but I was torn up inside and couldn't think straight. Now the decision was made for me and I didn't have to make that choice. I knew at that point it was over and I didn't know if I would ever see them again.  I saw Sue one more time before she did something that I could never have imagined.

# 9

## AN OCCUPATIONAL HAZARD

You would think that now would be the wakeup call for me but that is not what happened. I was full of anger and rage. After my court appearance, I'm sentenced to two years imprisonment and sent to Stafford Prison. I am twenty-two years old with a huge chip on my shoulder. I'm alone again; left out in the cold. Just like that first memory and the time in the Skegness cells when my dad had told the police to keep me there. This was all of my own doing but that was a bitter pill to swallow and I was much more inclined to find somebody else to blame, only this time I couldn't. This was it now and in a short time I would make a decision and that was…. "Fuck everyone and everything!" I was on my own and I was going to live my life any way I wanted and nobody could stop me.

My mates Mick, Tom and Steve, who had received their prison terms after I had been sent to the rehab, were about to finish their sentences and I was just starting mine. So in a few weeks, I was going to have no backup and would need to fend for myself. The two-year sentence that I had received meant that if I behaved myself I would only serve two-thirds of it and be freed in sixteen months. The eight months saved was called 'remission' and I could lose it if I misbehaved or caused problems so I decided to keep a low profile and get out as soon as possible.

That idea didn't last long. I soon started to get into trouble and lose remission and privileges such as 'association', which was to be let out of your cell in the evening to mix with the others and watch television or play some board games. I also learned what 'the block' was. It was the punishment block where they held people for more serious misbehaviour. My first trip there was for fighting. I had seen an inmate trying to force himself in a sexual way on a younger kid and I never thought twice about it and waded into him. I hated bullies. I am sure there was more to it than that; my own experiences of being coerced by a man to do something I didn't want to do surfaced and with it the rage. Whatever the reason, I could never have stood by and watched it happen. It did me a bit of good in one way as this guy had a bit of a reputation in the prison as a tough nut, so I gained some respect off the back of that for taking him on and we both went down the punishment block for a week.

It was all about pecking orders in there and you had no choice but to stand up for yourself or your life would be a misery of being picked on and bullied. Fortunately for me, my dad had imprinted his rage on me and it had come in useful on many occasions.

One thing about my upbringing that I am thankful for is that I never heard any racist or homophobic talk in our household and as a result I grew up with no prejudices around these areas. What I did build up over the years was an almost pathological hatred of paedophiles and prison became my hunting ground. They would try to mix in with the general population of the prison by lying about what their offences were but eventually the truth would come to light and we would be tipped off, sometimes by a prison officer (screw). It wasn't hard to find someone to accompany me as a lookout. I didn't feel bad about beating these people up and the next morning they would be outside the governor's office making an application to be put on 'Rule 43'. This is a protection wing that holds sex offenders, paedophiles and informers.

I wasn't long into my sentence when I was involved in a riot where most of the prison inmates sat in the exercise yard and refused to move. Some of those inmates had tried to help the Young Prisoners, all under-eighteens escape from their wing. They had barricaded themselves up against one end of the separate building they were housed in. I don't know how many inmates took part in this riot but there were a couple of hundred and it went on for two or three days. Every night, the prison officers were coming around and coaxing as many as possible to give up and so each morning we could see how successful they had been as the crowd was getting smaller and smaller. We had the bright idea that if we stuck together they wouldn't be able to put us all down the punishment block but we were in for a surprise. Once the numbers had been reduced enough for the prison officers to overpower us they rushed us and herded us into another building that unbeknown to us was being refurbished. They had a wing of empty cells there, one each for those of us who were still on the sit-in, which consisted of a mattress on the floor and a bucket to piss in. So much for our ideas about how this was going to turn out but to be honest the mattress was a bit of luxury after sleeping on the tarmac for two nights.

The next few days would be a procession of us appearing before the governor of the prison to have our remission taken off us. I can't remember how much I lost that day. Once we had seen the governor we were taken back to our original cells and normal prison life resumed.

I managed to get into a welding school that was being run in the prison grounds, so that was a plus. The instructor was a really nice man who taught me well and I received a City and Guilds certificate at the end of it. I did eventually start to use this time in prison to educate myself and started reading more books and taking classes. I had wasted my time at school and was starting to realise just how much I didn't know. I also started to realise that I wasn't stupid and very rarely failed a test when I put my mind to it.

Sometime near the end of my sentence, I was told that my wife, Sue wanted to see me and a special meeting through the Probation Service had been arranged without my knowledge. Sue had been brought to the prison for the meeting that day and I was taken out of my cell to see her. It was a shock to me and I refused; I didn't want to see her. It had been over a year since we had had any contact and I had no intentions of going back to her. I had made a decision that I was going back to what I knew. I believed that drugs were the only thing that made me feel half normal and so this was going to be my way of life. As much as I wanted my kids, I couldn't go back to Sue. I was put under a lot of pressure to see her that day but I still refused and as far as I was concerned it was over!

I had mixed feelings after they took me back to the cell. Anger was my constant companion and the anger was around that they had brought her to see me without asking me. I felt guilty that I had sent her away but seeing her would have been too painful and there was part of me that was relieved that it was over between us. I could always find a supply of cannabis in the prison when the feelings got too intense and this was one of those occasions.

At some point, I became eligible for parole. I had still managed to hold onto a couple of months of remission and I was told I could be released early. I told the parole board I didn't want the remission! I don't think they had had anyone turn down an opportunity to get out of prison early. The reason I turned it down was that I was under no illusions about what I would be doing when I got out and I didn't want any parole license hanging around my neck. I had even gone as far as planning which chemists I was going to break into first. I knew I could make a lot of money from what I did. I had lots of contacts in different parts of the country and I was now going to turn what I did into a career. Prison was now going to have to become an occupational hazard for me but I had no intentions of getting caught again.

I was excited at the prospect of being free again and the day finally arrived. It was around June 1973. I was met outside the prison gates by my friends, including Frizzel. Someone gave me some pills and I was high before we got out of Staffordshire. I remember stopping for a breakfast before the drugs kicked in and killed my appetite. Frizzel thought it would be a good idea to ask the waitress for an extra piece of bacon for me seeing as I had just got out of prison that morning! I don't think she saw the funny side of it but we did.

I went back to my mum and dad's house and after a few days I went to visit Sue and the kids. I didn't know it at the time but this was the last time I would see her. I would see Steven and my daughter Jane again but this would be the last time I would see Sue. I didn't know it at the time but I was about to be shipped out so to speak to another part of the country.

When I got back to Newark either on the first or second day I was offered a lift to an all-nighter at The Twisted Wheel in Manchester. On the journey, I realised that it was the same route that I had taken with my dad when we worked on Fiddlers Ferry but that seemed such a long time ago. Things took a turn for the worse. I realised that there were some people at the club who I had an altercation with before my prison sentence in which one of them had been quite badly beaten. Paranoia is one of the side effects of taking amphetamines also known as 'speed' and these guys started playing with my head by following me about or staring at me. I was so sure they were going to jump me and my night was ruined as I convinced myself that they were following us all the way home. Normally, I would have confronted them at the club but there was a part of me that was not in a hurry to go back to prison.

When I got back to my parents' house the following evening, I was still convinced the guys from the club were still following and watching me. I heard people coming down the passage between our house and next doors, climbing over the back gate. I was hearing voices. I can remember creeping downstairs and getting the carving knife out of the kitchen drawer going into my parents' room and standing in their front window that looked out onto the main road. It was eerie and by this time I was seeing things, too. I saw people in the shadows watching and waiting. I can't imagine how scared my parents were of me standing in their bedroom with this carving knife and talking to myself but I do remember my mum being that scared that she was physically sick. I eventually decided to confront whatever was out there and ended up on the street in just a pair of jeans with the knife shouting for these imagined or real people to show themselves. I must at some point have gone back in the house and back to bed.

I had only been home for a couple of days and my mum sprang into action the following day. They both went to see a friend of my dad's that I knew too called Charlie Harrison. He had connections in the power station industry and within a few days, I was put on a train with a suitcase, a bit of money and a ticket to Poole in Dorset. I didn't argue, I knew I had to get out of that town and at least give my parents a break.

I always have the memory of the train pulling into Poole and seeing the enormous blue harbour with the fishing boats and all the white buildings surrounding it. What a beautiful place. I didn't know anybody, I didn't know where I was going to stay and I was about to start a new job. Once I had found somewhere to stay, I made my way to that beautiful harbour and had a drink. On that very first night, I found someone that took me to a party where I was drinking and smoking cannabis. This was not what I planned but I was pretty screwed up with what had happened over the previous few days. I hadn't had a chance to acclimatise to outside life and here I was on the other side of the country trying to work things out. I always looked to a drug of some description when my head was messed up and this was no exception.

Things settled down a bit when I started work, although I did have a run-in with one of the locals I was working with who had somehow found out I had just got out of prison and thought he could call me 'the jailbird'. His name was called Caruso and I offered him out after work to settle this but thankfully he backed out. We became quite friendly and would go for a drink together after work. The power station isn't there anymore but it used to be within walking distance of Poole Quay and I loved spending my spare time there. One of the bars was called The Gas Tavern. Poole was renowned for big juicy cockles and The Gas Tavern was the place to get them. I would often find myself sitting in there after work with a pint of beer, a packet of cheese and onion crisps and a bowl of still warm Poole cockles. Bliss.

This period in my life was pretty settled and I was enjoying life for the first time in a long time. I was living in a nice bed and breakfast place and was starting to save a bit of money. It was mid-summer and I was spending time on the beach and going shopping in Bournemouth and visiting the New Forest. I felt truly free.

Then out of the blue, I was told that I was being transferred to another job. This wasn't unusual in the power industry. I was told I was being transferred to Havant in Hampshire to work on a new incinerator that was being built.

Just before I was due to leave, my brother Alan turned up. He had been working at Butlin's holiday camp in Clacton. I think he stayed in my digs for a couple of nights and then we went to Havant together and I managed to get him a job with me. He must have been eighteen by that time and so we began working together.

The manager let us stay at his lodgings where two or three others were staying too. It was owned by an Irish widowed lady who really looked after Alan and me, especially when she found out we were Catholic. She used to call us her 'boys' and would hide extra meat on our plates under eggs or other items. We were well spoilt but it wasn't the same as Poole. There was no quay or beautiful harbour to sit next to. We both started to drink more.

We would go to the local pub most nights on the pretext of taking the landlady's dog for a walk. After a few weeks the dog, an old Alsatian, would realise where it was going and park its backside and refuse to budge. We stopped taking it in the end. On a Saturday morning, we would buy a bottle of tequila and drink it in the park with the lemon and salt before we set out for the day.

There came a time while we were there when Alan had some problems during a night shift and had to be relieved. I am not sure what had happened; it might have been the results of our drinking habits. I think he told me he had been hallucinating and feeling panicked on the night shift. He went to the doctors and was given some medication. I remember being so incensed that he was taking these pills that I took them off him and flushed them down the toilet! Alan was shocked and incredulous that I- after all the drugs I had taken over the years- could get angry and flush his antidepressants down the loo. The thing was he was my only brother and I was scared he would follow in my footsteps. I was far from a good role model for him but I still felt responsible to keep him safe.

The biggest shock was about to come. I was tracked down by a social worker who told me that Sue had abandoned our two children on the desk of our local social security office in

Newark. They were due in court in a few days to have an interim care order and to be taken into a foster home.

I attended the court appearance but the judge told me there was no way the children could be released to me, after just coming out of prison. Jane and Steven went to a foster home, where I hoped they would be safe. Alan would travel with me on the train to see them most weekends.

Eventually, this job in Havant came to an end and we moved back to Bournemouth.

# 10
# THE IMMACULATE
# CONTRACTION

We are back in Bournemouth and I am not
sure how it came about but now there were
six of us: Pat, Ginnely, Fluff, Loftus, Alan and
myself. Fluff and Alan had their girlfriends
with them- Isabel and Bernie- who they had
met on their stay at Butlin's. We went looking
for a place to rent and managed to find a large
house that had previously been a guest house
that was within walking distance of the sea
and perfectly suited our needs down to the
ground.

We had some good times in that
Bournemouth guesthouse. Alan and Fluff had
their girlfriends but Pat and I were free agents
and were having a whale of a time with the
different girls down on holiday who just
wanted to have some fun.  Every week or so

some girls would leave and new ones would arrive; those summer months were a special time for us. Pat was about twenty years old, with a wonderful sense of humour. We both had long hair and were tanned from all the hours on the beach. I was a bit older than the others by about five years.

Figure 4 - Trevor & Pat, Bournemouth, 1976

We were spending lots of time meeting different girls and just having fun. Sometimes if we didn't get too drunk we might get lucky and they would come back to our guesthouse. I was happy and loving this life that mainly consisted of spending all our spare time on the beach, sunbathing and swimming and in the evenings going to clubs and pubs. What more could I ask for? It was like being on permanent holiday- except for the work part of it- but what I was earning on Poole Power Station was paying for this lifestyle.

I did come unstuck on one of my encounters with the carefree holidaymakers when Pat and I met a couple of Geordie girls and they came back to the house with us. After a short while Pat's girl went upstairs with him but mine was reluctant and I thought I had lost my touch but she revealed to me that she was a virgin and that was the reason she didn't want to sleep with me. I eventually talked her around and we spent the night together. I was feeling pretty pleased with myself that this girl had chosen me to lose her virginity to but it was to be short-lived because a few days later I was being treated for an STD! You can imagine how shocked I was and how much piss-taking I was getting from the lads at the house. In keeping with my Catholic upbringing, I decided to name it 'the immaculate contraction'.

Another embarrassment was that I had to contact anyone I had slept with after this girl and a day or so before an ex-girlfriend from Newark had dropped in and stopped the night on her way to Weymouth to catch a ferry to Jersey to start a new life. I had to contact her to tell her that she needed to have a check-up and she might have an STD. I didn't want to make that call but knew I had to. It felt so shameful and embarrassing.

I was going back to working at Poole Power Station every year, where they would do the usual annual maintenance work but as with all power station work, it was only seasonal. So in the winter not only did I not have much money but the town turned into a ghost town. I did manage to pick up a bit of cash-in-the-hand work with a roofer doing repair work on a bunch of flat roofs and he gave Alan and Pat a job too, so this gave us a bit of extra cash.

During this time I had still been taking trips back to Newark on the train to see my children and Alan would often come with me. They were with their foster parents, and lived on a local estate in a council house. The house was always clean and they had a collie dog and a small but tidy garden. The man of the house was a big man and worked as an ambulance driver, the woman was small and dumpy but seemed nice enough. I would make arrangements to take Jane and Steven out for the day and spoil them when I could and that would all revolve around when I was working and had money.

When it came to dropping them back at the house, they would always cry when it was time for me to leave. It was so heartbreaking to see them so upset. They were so little; Jane was only two and Steve was five. I always felt that they were safe in that house or I would have found a way to get them out. It wasn't until much later- in fact after the foster mother had died- that I found out that she had a problem around women and as a result, Jane was being physically and emotionally abused and badly treated.

The thing was, I had been to see the foster mother in the nursing home where she had been taken just before she died and told her how much it meant to me that she had taken good care of the children when I couldn't. I was so angry when I finally found out what the truth was and not only that, she had told Steve and Jane other lies but I don't want to get in front of myself.

It was never good for me to be in Newark too long because I would always end up taking drugs. I am not sure what we were doing in Bournemouth, we were drinking a lot and smoking cannabis and taking acid (LSD) now and again.

I had taken LSD quite a few times but the most recent times had turned into a bad trip where I saw myself die in a car accident…. I am trapped in the car after it leaves the road and crashes. It is dark. I am alone and can feel myself slowly bleeding to death and there is no one to help me. After this first trip, I had taken another some months later and it had taken me back to this same scene of being trapped and bleeding to death. I even felt my heart coming to a stop and travelling to another dimension, or heaven or something and meeting my brother Graham and talking to him. When I eventually came around I was confused and not sure what was real and what was imagined because it all seemed so real. I think I had freaked my friends out because most of this happened in a car on a trip to the coast. At one point they had stopped the car to try to calm me down.

I don't know what would have possessed me to try it again but they do say the definition of insanity is doing the same thing and expecting a different result. So I took LSD again and this time it very nearly did kill me. My friend Pat and I decided to take a trip of acid as it was a beautiful summer's day, we had a couple of girls with us but it wasn't long before my trip started to turn dark.

I don't know why but I had a flood of feelings and memories from my past. I just had this overwhelming feeling of despair and hopelessness. It was a tsunami of blackness, with all the memories of what had happened to me mixed with all the things I had done. I had fulfilled my dad's prophecy of "You will never amount to anything as long as you have a hole in your arse". I had my mum's words ringing in my ears that "It should have been you that got killed not Graham". I had let everyone down. My kids were in care. I was either drinking or taking drugs and had become this monumental waste of space. I thought the best thing I could do was kill myself. This wasn't a passing thought. This was an all-consuming, overpowering uncompromised decision that was made; this is what will happen today. There was no doubt in my mind and I wasn't frightened by what I was going to do. It felt as if I had been given a commandment.

One of my worst fears was of only being this pathetic creature that would eventually die of an overdose and be found in a squalid flat some days later and maybe with a small reference to it in the corner of the local paper. So, I decided that my ending was going to be something special. It was going to be a spectacular event that would be splashed all over the front pages of the newspapers. I had this crazy plan and my first stop with my three friends in tow was the local Bournemouth Echo office in the centre of town. I had the bright idea to get a reporter, camera in hand, to interview me and take pictures and don't tell me how I managed it but I got one to come with us. As I remember it, the newspaper office was below a multi-storey car park and as we made our way up he followed and I explained my reasons for doing it and why he must document it.

There was a non-negotiable determination to do this as all these unrelenting dark thoughts continued to overpower me. Everyone was trying to make me see sense but I wasn't listening. I felt that this was my salvation in some way and there was no turning back. The girl I was with was hysterical and desperately trying to talk me out of it but it was to no avail. Eventually the reporter backed out and as much as I tried to change his mind he refused to go any further. I remember feeling so disappointed but it just meant that now I had to think of something else.

Shortly after this, I decided I needed to finish this quickly and so I put my head under the rear wheel of a bus as it stopped at a bus stop in the centre of Bournemouth. I just wanted the thoughts to stop and I remember the bus started to move but someone had jumped out of his car and dragged me out in the nick of time and it was the nick of time because when it moved the wheel had taken a small patch of my scalp off.

I wasn't happy with the outcome and proceeded to berate this poor man who had literally saved my life. At this point I had completely lost my mind and was running over the top of cars on the road just generally running amok and feeling so frightened because by now I was being chased by the police. It wasn't long before they had me cornered and arrested me. I can remember going crazy in the police station and insisting that I was Jesus (!) and other nonsense. They held me overnight and by then the LSD had worn off. I was lucky enough to only be charged with violent behaviour in a police station and in February 1976 received a £10 fine. I don't think those policemen realised it but if they hadn't locked me up that day, I don't think I would be writing about this today.

When I arrived home my friends looked more than a little sheepish and wanted to know what happened but I never told them what had really been going off in my head after all I didn't want them to think I was any crazier than they already did and so I just put it down to a bad trip. Pat later confided in me that one of the most worrying things for him was that I nearly convinced him it was a good idea.

We eventually left the house on St Michael's Road and moved into a large flat in

Westbourne on the outskirts of Bournemouth. We were a rowdy bunch and now and then would take the bus to town for a night out. It was normal for us to be singing at the top of our voices and (although I imagine we were quite annoying) we were never nasty. It was all meant to be in good fun but unfortunately we could sometimes find ourselves attracting unwanted attention.

Here are a couple of those incidents that come to mind... One evening after we had been to a club in Poole some of the local lads had decided they didn't like us and followed us after we left. It was just Pat, Alan, Fluff and myself and we arrived at a fish and chip shop in the town where they caught up with us. There were a few insults going backwards and forwards and I was just leaning against a wall watching this develop and starting to escalate when my brother Alan intervened and stepped forward to try and defuse the situation. I was towards the back listening with amusement but it went something like this "Look lads, there is no need for this. We are all out in our best clothes and if we start fighting they are going to get torn and have blood on them and nobody wants that do we? What I suggest is that you pick your best fighter and my brother will fight him!" We still laugh about it to this day but it was effective because we all went our separate ways.

There were quite a few incidents like this but the worst one happened in the flat. It was St Patrick's Day and our friend Pat was an Irish Catholic whose birthday was the same day and we had been out celebrating and returned to the flat where the party continued. Pat insisted on playing The Dubliners on the record player really loudly. As a result, the neighbours came down complaining about it. I remember going to the door and seeing this little crowd of irate neighbours and assured them I would turn it down and they went, but Pat wanted it back on again and turned it back up. This was followed by banging on the door again and as I opened the door for the second time I was hit in the jaw with a tube of some description and I couldn't see the damage but the blood was pouring down my t-shirt.

At this point, all hell broke and the biggest of the bunch threw the one with the pole into the room with me. At one point I had tried to throw him out of the first-floor window but someone else had joined in. I was now in full-on survival mode and in a blind panic I stamped on his head, knocking him out. I was now in the small toilet area with the big guy but he soon changed his mind when he realised that I had lost the plot and he wanted out and asked me to let him go which I did. The police arrived and when I looked around it was just carnage. Alan was laid on top of a door that had been knocked off its hinges; people in different rooms and blood was all over the walls that unfortunately was mostly mine. I was just starting to realise how much blood I had lost, as I looked down to see a 'v shape' bloodstain that had spread across my t-shirt the width of my chest and was now soaking into my underwear.

I just sat there in shock as a paramedic worked on me. While this was happening, I noticed the guy who I had stamped on and had done this to me was coming around and being arrested.

I was taken to the hospital and stitched up. I learned that the metal tube had entered just below my bottom lip and gone through and broken three teeth off and they were still attached to the jaw bone. They stitched my lip up inside and out and I was sent home and returned the following day to have a brace put in and wired up to hold the broken jaw in place. I looked like a mess and it took a few months to start looking better.

While at this flat I had attempted to break into a couple of local chemists. They were both disasters. The first one was not far from the flat in Westbourne. I had checked it out and saw that it closed on a Thursday afternoon and that around the back was hidden from view and had easy to access sash windows. So

I picked my day and everything went ok. I entered the first-floor window and just as I was about to make my way down the stairs into the shop area when I heard a vacuum cleaner being switched on! I never thought about cleaners being in there and I made a quiet but hasty retreat.

The next one wasn't much better. It was in the town centre and I had found one chemist with a flat roof at the back leading to a window with outside bars on it but these were usually just a frame bolted into the wall. I decided to do this one just after closing time, the reason being if anyone heard noises they wouldn't be too concerned about it. So I am on the flat roof and have undone the bolts on the barred frame and about to put it on the ground when a light comes on and the Pharmacist steps out of an office and into the corridor and I am stood at the other end in full view but luckily he didn't see me and leaves. I wait a few minutes and proceed to break in. I can't remember why but I only come away with a few things off the shelves and have to leave without finding the main drugs cabinet. I was losing my touch.

I don't know when we left that flat and went our separate ways but Pat and I had started dating two local girls Trisha and Bridgett. Trisha and I were together for a few years. It was the first long term relationship I had had since my marriage ended.

Trisha and I decided that we would have a holiday abroad and I had heard of a bus that hippies used to travel and it was called the 'Magic Bus'. We agreed to give it a go. We decided to go to Greece and do some island hopping. I expected it was going to be a psychedelic bus, but when we arrived at the Victoria Station Bus Terminal in London, I was disappointed to find it was just a normal bus.

We had open returns, which meant we could travel back any time within twelve months. The tickets cost around £70 and the journey would take a little over three days. We would be camping to save money and so were both carrying rucksacks. The bus was very comfortable with air conditioning and I could see this being a nice relaxed and easy three days. We were about to be surprised, when we reached Paris and told we would be transferred to another bus for the rest of the journey to Athens. We got our belongings together and went to this other bus and saw it was nothing like the one we had just left. It was old and beat up and there were no mod cons; the air conditioning was accessed by opening a window! Along the way we would pick people up and drop them off; they sometimes would have chickens and small animals that they carried in cages. I think this was a way of the Greek drivers making a bit of extra money on the trip.

The journey was tiresome, but eventually we arrived in Athens. We still had to get to the islands. I think we stayed in a youth hostel for the night and took in a few sites. Piraeus was a busy port and as we walked down the streets we would see exotic dancers with snakes around their necks trying to entice us into the bars and clubs. We made our way back to the hostel before setting off the following morning to Poros, our island destination. We finally arrived and it was quite stunning with the white buildings and the blue sea. We left the ferry and walked out of the town around the coast to find a beach to camp on. We didn't have to walk for long before we found one and set up our camp. Unbeknown to us we had chosen a nudist beach so you can imagine the shock on our faces to get up the next morning to find all these naked people walking around, after a while with the help of a little ouzo our inhibitions fell away and we followed suit and I found it quite freeing.

We had some friends join us that had flown in, my friend, Pat came so did Brian and his girlfriend, Lizzy with her daughter, Janine who would have been about seven at the time. We were living a hippy lifestyle of swimming and sunbathing and drinking ouzo. We were about a couple of miles out of town so each morning a couple of us would walk into town and buy fresh bread. We could smell the bread before we could see the bakery and together with cheese, this became our staple diet, mixed with the local foods such as Souvlaki (grilled octopus) that were hung to dry on racks by the harbour and together with a bit of campsite cooking and lots of salad, this was how we lived.

It was great to watch little Janine walking about this nudist beach and talking to strangers and it didn't seem to make any difference to her what language they used, she would just chat away without a care in the world. I guess she was showing me something I longed for and that was to not have a care in the world and, yes, it was easier for me to like that in a place like this. It was a different proposition back in the real world. Back there I was riddled with feelings of restlessness, irritability, insecurities and discontentment. I would get fleeting glimpses of how life could be- like in that moment with Janine- but I couldn't hold on to them.

We were all having a wonderful time on this beautiful island but I ended up falling out with Trisha over something silly. I had seen her laughing and joking with my friend Pat after we had argued and that brought all my insecurities to the surface following Sue cheating on me. I had a cruel trait that I used whenever I felt emotionally hurt and that was no matter what someone might have said or done to hurt me I would go out of my way to hurt them more. I said some terrible things to Trisha and she decided to go home and to my shame I let her do that three-day journey on her own. I stayed for another couple of weeks and then went back to Bournemouth. We had originally arrived in Athens with £180 and I left the island five weeks later. Despite my behaviour towards the end, we had a fantastic holiday and I have some wonderful memories of those days.

# 11
# THE JOB AT USAF ALCONBURY

Trish and I managed to get back together and we went to live in Southsea for a while after I was asked to go back and do some more work on Havant Incinerator. We found a small bedsitter to stay in. I was mostly drinking and had started smoking more dope at that time and occasionally using speed. The job was only for a few months and eventually came to an end.

When we came back to Bournemouth from Southsea, we moved into a quite beautiful ground-floor flat that looked out over a large lawn and garden. At the end of the garden were a number of trees. It had wildlife in the grounds and we had a squirrel that would tap on the French windows for food. The flat had two bedrooms, a large living room and kitchen but what I found equally attractive about this flat was that it was furnished with beautiful antique furniture. It even had a table in the living room that had a poster on the underneath saying it had been in the possession of Admiral Nelson at some point. The man that owned the building was a lovely old gentleman and so friendly.

While we were staying there, I was offered a job at an American air base in Cambridgeshire called Alconbury for a firm called Carter Horsley. I would be working away from home and travelling back to Bournemouth at the weekends. The job at Alconbury involved the building of enormous blast-proof doors to fit on the aircraft hangers. It was going to be a long job, well paid and had a strong trade union presence. You had to be a paid-up union member to work on that site and our shop steward was a man called Alfie Walford. He was well versed in trade union matters and a tough negotiator. I had a lot of admiration and respect for him.

I rented a caravan on a nice clean site next to the dog track in Peterborough. I had an old 650cc BSA motorbike and sidecar at the time and travelled backwards and forwards to work in it. The Americans would often come and look at the bike and try and buy it off me. They were big fans of old English motorcycles and wanted to take them back to the States. We were allowed to use the facilities on the site and ate in their NAAFI and we also had access to their clubhouse, which had discos on certain nights. While at Alconbury, I met Barry who became a good friend and he was travelling to Ringwood in Hampshire, which was only a few miles outside Bournemouth, and so we started travelling together. Barry was quite a character with his mop of black curly hair and his Dorset accent. He had such a sense of humour and amongst the many incidents, one that stands out was this one: Barry was always pleading poverty and one of the contractors had believed him, took pity on him and started bringing extra sandwiches into work to share with him. This went on for months until one day this guy took out the sandwiches and as Barry picked one up he said "What, fucking egg, again". Well, all hell broke loose and the table went over and nearly ended up in a fight until Barry convinced the man he was only joking.

I really liked Barry. He would put on his Dorset accent and act like he wasn't very smart but he was as sharp as a razor. He lived in a beautiful cottage in the middle of the New Forest where he restored vintage cars. I would visit him every now and again and we went out on his boat fishing in the Solent. We are still in touch and I still visit him every now and again.

This was a good job for me and I was keeping out of trouble and although I was still using drugs it wasn't chaotic and I was managing to hold it together. Unfortunately, this was all about to change.

After about a year something happened and I can't remember the exact details but the management wanted to change the terms and conditions of our contract. That would mean a cut in our wages, so a union meeting was called and we voted to go on strike. This was around 1977 and Margaret Thatcher was waging war on the trade unions. We had formed a picket line that was manned seven days a week. It was a time when picket lines were restricted to six picketers. Flying pickets were banned, meaning other union members who wanted to show their solidarity with us could not travel from other parts of the country to support us and you were not allowed to try and stop anyone crossing the picket line.

This was not the case for us... We had hundreds of union members from all over the country come to support us including many from the London docks. So, not only had we flooded the main entrance with these flying pickets but the six picketers to a picket line law was broken. We then had a police presence trying to enforce these new laws and so we agreed to only have six on the gate and the rest were classed as supporters.

This went on for a number of weeks and we were mostly interested in stopping any materials for our job going onto the site. A lot of other vehicles were being turned away and not always by us, some were union members themselves and weren't prepared to cross a picket line. Every now and again the police would arrest someone for trying to intimidate a driver but mostly it ran smoothly. Anyone who had been arrested was brought before Huntingdon Magistrates' Court and that day would be chaos. The tiny court would be flooded with protesters and even the court officials had a hard time getting into the court house and this happened quite a few times over the weeks.

Things started to escalate after that first couple of weeks and we had been told that the company was intending to bring workers from Italy to do our job. This was known as 'scab labour' and so there seemed to be a bigger presence of men and an angry atmosphere on that day. It wasn't long before two or three mini buses of these Italian workers arrived at the gate and it seemed as if all hell broke loose. There was no way those buses were going through that gate and I don't know if it was a plan or not but there was a distraction created at the back of the base and when the police went to intervene, a number of burly dockers grabbed the bottom of the three buses and flipped them on their sides and it happened so quickly the police didn't have a clue who had done it.

The van was righted somehow and the Italian workers went home. I remember how shook up they looked and felt a little sorry for them. I heard that the Union made contact with the Italian Communist Party about those workers trying to break our picket line and I don't know what they did about it but we never saw any more try to get through after that.

This was turning out to be a long strike and so we started to organise ourselves and build a rota where we would take it in turns to do picket duty. The Union also organised a strike fund, where other sites throughout the country would collect money to put in the fund to support us and we would get a payment when we turned up for picket duty. The media were getting involved and we would often have reporters and the odd film crew come to see what it was all about.

Barry and I would travel from Bournemouth to the Alconbury site that was nearly two hundred miles and do our picket duty. The manager at the local hotel knew us because we had used his bar after work in the past, and so he would let us put a tent up at the back of the hotel while we were picketing. This was to go on for nine or ten weeks and during that time I was going to be drawn back- about fifty miles further up the A1 from Alconbury – to Newark.

I had been back to Newark a couple of times while I was still working for the odd night out at The Bowling Green, Newark's one and only night club. I was gradually spending more time there as the strike dragged on. It was about this time that I started to use 'Class A' drugs and the first one I tried was morphine. I can remember the day clearly. I had been staying with my friend, Brian who had a rented caravan near a local river. I had met up with Kevin, the guy I had met in rehab. He had some ampules (injectables) of morphine and was telling us how amazing this was and so I tried it and from that first injection I was hooked. I hadn't been getting the same effect from the speed for some time but this was a whole new level and from that first injection I had stepped onto a rollercoaster that I couldn't get off of and would stay on for the following twenty years.

It wouldn't be long after this that I was back to breaking into chemists. I have to be careful about what I write in here and I am only talking about chemists that I have been charged with. Although this happened a long time ago and I don't think anyone would come looking for me after all this time, the United Kingdom is one of the few countries that doesn't have a statute of limitations, so in theory I could be charged if I say anything that incriminates me. I have only been charged with a small number of the chemists I broke into. I would imagine that the real numbers must be pushing a hundred or more, all over the country.

This next fiasco was a real comedy of errors. I found myself on a train to King's Cross at 7am in the morning with my friend, Frizzel who had the proceeds of a chemist in a rucksack that he was carrying. When we arrived at the station it only took just over an hour to get to London. We removed some drugs prior to putting the rucksack in the left luggage. Some were for our own use but we also needed some money and so we went to Piccadilly to sell some of our drugs and raise a bit of cash. It didn't take long but we noticed that we were attracting too much attention and grabbed a black cab and went back to King's Cross.

We took a room in a hotel directly opposite the station and then we made a phone call and invited a couple of girls from Newark that we knew to join us. The night was spent using drugs and a bit of paranoia was setting in so regular checking out of the window was happening. We were on the ground floor and just a little way up from us was a parked black cab and it stayed there all night. We were getting a bit nervous so the next morning when we went down for breakfast we asked the owner and he informed us that the night before the hotel had been held up by an armed gang and robbed!

So, in all of London we had managed to pick perhaps the only hotel that had had an armed robbery the night before and I am sure our constant curtain twitching during the night had not gone unnoticed and sure enough it hadn't. We collected our few belongings and stepped out onto the street and it wasn't long before we realised we were being followed.

So, now the fear of being caught is rising and so it is all about escaping. The first thing we do is discreetly pass the all-important left luggage ticket and any drugs we had to the girls and told them to go home and we would lead the police away. It eventually turned into a chase and my first instinct is to climb onto a roof where I feel safer and at the same time we can hear police sirens as they closed in on us. Opposite the flat roof I found myself on was a block of flats with verandas and a girl must have realised my predicament and was beckoning me to come across to the veranda. I passed her my bag but it was too far to jump, I just thought I would be safe once in her flat. She told me to come around the front. I had a small wall in front of me and I vaulted over it. What I didn't realise was that on the other side was a glass skylight and I went straight through it landing in a shower of glass, luckily in between two rows of desks with office girls who were sitting working on computers. I just remember jumping up brushing myself off and greeting them with a cheery "Good morning!" and walking out the front door. The look on their faces was priceless!

I didn't even look for the flat, I just ran and ended up back at King's Cross. I don't know where Mick is at this point but I am just running in a blind panic. I manage to find a stairway that leads to another roof and I am running on a slate roof that was slippery with transport police chasing me and I am goading them shouting "Come on, lads, keep up!", so the drugs must be still working! I manage to avoid them and end up down in the train station again and my only escape is to cross the lines where I can see a wall that I can scale and so off I go and I manage to reach the wall and so my escape is imminent, but when I reach the top of the wall, which was about seven or eight foot on my side, it was about thirty foot on the other side and, suddenly, it was over. I climbed down and was arrested and transported to Clerkenwell Police Station.

Things got a bit out of hand at the police station and I realised that because there had been an alert about IRA activity the police had thought we were terrorists. When they realised we weren't they were far from happy and started to question me. Mick had also been caught and was in the next cell. Neither of us had anything on us although they did find one tablet on me that I had missed. So the questioning started. I had no intention of telling them anything and I knew it was going to get rough but I knew how to play this game; this was only another form of my dad's belt so I just battened down the hatches and refused to answer any questions. I thought if I just kept quiet they would eventually have to bail us out.

I was no stranger to police beatings in custody; it had happened in most of my arrests, sometimes due to my smart mouth. I enjoyed goading them but these London Metropolitan Police were a different breed and I was beaten so badly that I lost the use of my legs. I heard them go next door to Mick's cell and he just caved in and told them his details straight away. He was a bit that way inclined and he told me afterwards he didn't want a taste of what he had just heard me go through.

Anyway, after a while they realised I wasn't faking not being able to stand up and had to call an ambulance. I was taken to the nearest hospital where they diagnosed a suspected ruptured spleen and I was admitted and put on a ward where I was handcuffed to a bed and had my own personal babysitter in the form of a police officer who sat at the end of the bed.

There had been a lot of publicity recently at that time about a guy called Liddle Towers. He had died in police custody in County Durham of a ruptured spleen. So now I would try and use this to my advantage and was calling myself 'Trevor Liddle Towers'. I told the police officer that if they gave me bail I wouldn't press charges and the charges they had on me at the time were not serious ones. Eventually it was agreed and I was bailed to appear at court at a later date. The hospital was trying to talk me out of signing myself out and saying I could have internal bleeding but I wasn't listening and left.

There was only one flaw in my 'cunning plan' and that was that I couldn't walk and I had no money. I managed to get outside by using anything I could to support me and then find a phone. I had one chance, the only person I knew in London and I didn't know how far away he was but I rang him. It was Alfie Walford, our shop steward. I will never forget how relieved I was when he said "Stay where you are I will come and fetch you".

When he picked me up I couldn't thank him enough. He took me back to where he lived and I remember it being a multi-storey block of flats and the lift was broken so he had to give me a fireman's carry up a number of flights of stairs. He took me into his family home and put me in a bath, washed and dressed me and put me to bed. I don't know how long I was there but while I was there he had asked me what had happened, and he just asked me not to say anything about drugs. I suspect his family wouldn't appreciate him bringing a drug addict into their home and it wasn't something I would have said anything about anyway.

I was slowly getting the use of my legs back and I was able to walk with the aid of a walking stick and Alfie put me on the train at Waterloo Station back to Bournemouth. When I got back to the flat and Trisha, I thought I could relax but I was to learn that the police were looking for me regarding a chemist burglary in Newark. I was arrested shortly afterwards and transported back to Newark where I was questioned about the chemist and denied any involvement. It seems Mick had been brought in for questioning and admitted his part and also implicated me in some way. I was out on bail again but eventually charged with the break in.

I think Mick knew he owed me big time for dropping me in it so I got a share of the drugs that had been retrieved from London and I then went back to Bournemouth for some rest and recuperation. Well, that is what I thought but I was in for a surprise and it wasn't going to be a good one!

# 12
## THE DAY MY MUM DIED

My life was spiraling out of control and I didn't seem to care. My relationship with Trish was coming to an end and the stress of trying to deal with my behaviour was making her ill. I was starting to go missing more often and using more drugs. Trisha never used drugs and had tolerated my on-and-off using around her but now things escalated. She learned about London and what I had been up to and it all became too much for her. It was about this time I had a message from Alfie, our shop steward, saying that the strike was over and the company had agreed to pay us around £2000 compensation and I was to be at a place near the site to collect it in person.

The day came and I found myself in a hotel room close to the venue with my brother, Alan. It was the day before I was due to pick up the cheque. I was still on crutches and we were both using the drugs that Mick had given us. On that night, my brother overdosed in the hotel room and I can remember trying to keep him awake and walking him around the room most of the night. He eventually came out of it. I remember that night so clearly because during that time I had a million and one things going through my mind, such as what if he dies and then I am responsible for both my brothers dying. Should I call an ambulance? I decided not to because I didn't want the police involved. It worked out ok in the end but it could easily have gone the other way.

My life was a series of trying to get away with things and in that moment I realised the great extent I would go to to save myself and avoid the consequences. I had risked my only brother's life that night but the next morning I carried on as if nothing had happened, convincing myself that it wasn't that serious and then stuffing it away with all the multitude of other things I didn't want to look at. I was living in a fantasy world as some sort of James Dean character but this one was more of 'a rebel without a clue'.

I collected my cheque, had a chat with Alfie and a few of the lads and was also told that we had all got our jobs back as part of the deal. I was on my merry way and things were looking up and maybe I could settle things down a bit. I knew I had those pending court cases to deal with, so this was on my mind.

The first one to come around was the one at Clerkenwell Magistrates' Court. They weren't serious charges and amounted to a few fines; one was for trespass on British Rail property and another for possession of a Class C drug, mandrax, which was a sedative and not on the list of drugs taken from the Newark chemist. That fact would help me at my next trial.

That trial at Nottingham Crown Court came up and as usual I would show up suited and booted and I was fairly confident of the outcome. Mick had already been convicted and sentenced, I knew he would never give evidence against me and the rest was circumstantial and so I was found not guilty. During the trial the jury isn't allowed to know anything about any past convictions but once the trial is over they can be told. After the verdict was read out, the judge asked the prosecutor "Has Mr Tacey any previous convictions for chemist burglaries?" and the prosecutor answered, "Yes" and the judge asked, "Could you read out the last one?" and it was only the same chemist! I remember seeing the jurors' faces and they were far from happy! It reminded me of what it might have been like to look into the faces of a lynch mob.

This would have been an ideal opportunity for me to get my life back on track but as usual I sabotaged it all. I was back working at Alconbury Air Base and living in my caravan at Peterborough and I still had the motorbike and sidecar. A memory that comes to mind concerning the motorbike and sidecar was riding through Peterborough, the bike was an old BSA 650cc with a big two-seater sidecar on it and painted bright red, so you can imagine it was quite an eye-catcher. Anyway, as I was driving through the town I noticed a group of young girls looking at me and I was smiling at them, revving the bike a bit and generally showing off when I suddenly looked back to the road and saw that the car in front had stopped at the traffic lights. The road was wet from a recent downpour and as I frantically applied the brakes I skidded around in a perfect one hundred and eighty degree circle, avoiding the car in front but completely facing in the opposite direction as the next car pulled up and boxed me in. Well, the girls I had been trying to impress at this time were in fits of laughter. I managed to manoeuvre myself into facing the right way and make a hasty but red-faced retreat.

I realise now that I had periods of my life that were relatively stable with a sense of contentment but after a while there was a part of me that would destroy it all. I felt as if something was lying dormant inside of me and then at some point it wakes up and destroys anything I might have built or cared about. I felt as if I was some kind of human wrecking ball. The periods of some sense of stability were getting shorter and the chaotic times were getting more frequent and lasting longer. I was also becoming even more self-centred and had little concern for anyone else.

Alconbury was coming to an end and so was my relationship with Trish. I was to return to Newark and Trish and I would part our ways. At this time, I had a small trunk that housed everything I owned, which consisted of a few clothes, a few books and some record albums. I was now nearly always injecting my drugs and using amphetamines and opiates mostly and it was fast becoming a daily occurrence.

I was back in Newark and I was quickly getting involved with all things drug related. Hash was a big thing at the time so I started acquiring hash with exotic names like Kashmir, Moroccan, Thai sticks, and Nepalese. We were coming through the Hippy era and not only had my taste in music changed- I was now listening to Pink Floyd, Patti Smith, Van Morrison, The Doors- but I also had a new set of friends. These were mostly Alan's friends and were about five years younger than me. My generation were all settled down and building family lives and some had just moved away from my craziness or they were in prison. One of the good things about being known to always have drugs available is you get invited to lots of parties. I was also getting attention from quite a few girls who seemed to be attracted to my bad boy image.

Figure 5 - Trevor's motorbike

There was a lot of synthetic amphetamine (speed) on the streets at this time and a lot of people were turning to this. Some of it was in powder form and some in tablets known as 'Backstreet Blues'. It was very much hit and miss quality-wise and if you found a good dealer, you usually stuck with him. I was also buying heroin off a dealer. This wasn't pharmaceutical; it was imported and known as 'Brown' because that's what colour it was. I soon became tired of buying my drugs and it wasn't long before I was back to my old trade. I was staying at various friends' houses and so I had no fixed abode and so it was harder to be tracked down, if anyone was looking for me. It seemed to work well and I was moving around constantly. If the police were looking for me sometimes Alan would get mistaken for me and be bundled off to the police station. I thought it was quite amusing but it couldn't have been much fun for him.

Things got pretty busy really quick and it wasn't long before I was getting visitors from four or five surrounding counties to see what I had. I managed to avoid getting caught for about eight months and then had another crown court appearance for a chemist break in. I am not sure how I got caught but ended up with a six month suspended sentence for two years.

Just four months later, here I am at Warwick Crown Court and have been on remand in Winson Green Prison- the worst prison I have been in- and I am sentenced to two years imprisonment. These were virtually straight after each other because I had been on remand for at least two months. A short time later I would be taken back to Nottingham Crown Court from Winson Green to face another a pending charge where I had been involved in an incident involving one of Mick's relatives who had asked Mick and I to help him with a problem around his wife's lover and it ended in violence. This was the first time I had violence on my record but that was more luck than judgement. We were sentenced to a further eight months each but the judge made it concurrent and so it ran alongside the original two year sentences we were already serving, thank goodness. We were back at Lincoln Prison and pleased to be out of Winson Green. Mick and I had managed to get a cell together when one evening the door was opened and there stood the prison chaplain. This wasn't unusual because sometimes he would come around and have a chat with the inmates but that wasn't the case this time he called me outside and told me that my dad had died that day. I was put back in the cell and I just went crazy. I was crying and smashing things up in the cell. Mick stayed clear of me; he knew better than to try and calm me down but eventually I did and laid there, full of remorse.

Over the next couple of days, I had to make an application to the governor of the prison to be allowed to go to the funeral and it was agreed that I could. I was relieved that I was able to go but there was also the shame and humiliation of being taken by a prison guard and handcuffed. When the day came we arrived at the church in a taxi. I had my own clothes on and the guard was in his civilian clothes. Just before we got out of the taxi he turned to me and said, "I will take the handcuffs off but you have to promise me you won't do anything stupid". I promised and I knew that I wouldn't do anything that would hurt or shame my family further and I hugged my mum before we went into the church.

My dad was buried in the same plot as my brother, Graham. The guard had allowed me to travel in the main car following the hearse while he travelled at the back in the taxi. As I stood there at the graveside watching my dad's coffin being lowered into the grave, I felt a great loss and wished I could have been with him at the end. I was thinking of all the things I wanted to say to him and all the anger I had had towards him seemed to melt away into insignificance at that point but it would resurface over time.

After the burial, everyone went back to my mum's house and the guard allowed me to go. He was a kind and thoughtful man and had taken a big chance trusting me but I had no intentions of doing anything that would cause anyone a problem. I was allowed to go where I liked in the house and even allowed a few glasses of whisky and there was food but eventually it was time to go back to prison and we all said a tearful goodbye to each other.

Sometime later my brother told me that he had been with my dad the day before he died and the last words he said to him was "I hope our Trevor sorts himself out". Those words would stay with me and I did sort myself out but it was going to take about another fifteen years.

Prison life for me was about trying to keep out of trouble but not tolerating any nonsense from anyone. It was not hard to get drugs in prison. It was mostly cannabis but there were syringes about and diabetics were a good source. When on remand there were lots of opportunities and because you could have your own food brought there was a steady supply coming in on almost a daily basis. Now and again someone would get caught but it just meant that the visitors would come up with more ingenious ways to fool the guards. I never asked anyone to do this for me but I knew plenty of people that did. It was a constant search for people who had just had a visit and were likely to have smuggled something. Then it was just a matter of leaning on them a little with empty promises to get a share.

Once we were sentenced and moved to the main prison with a visit allowed once a month and nothing allowed in, except books and magazines that had to be posted, it became a lot more difficult but not impossible. Letters were important in prison and except for the occasional visit this was our only contact with the outside world. I was still in contact with a couple of ex-girlfriends and a couple of mates and would wait with anticipation at lunch when the mail came round. It was a real disappointment when nothing arrived.

I don't know when it happened, it might have been after the funeral but I stopped using drugs in prison and I started signing up for the educational classes. I had no educational qualifications from school and although my Maths was always pretty good, my English was atrocious. I was embarrassed by my inability to write and spell. Something else that changed was that I was asking the prison librarian for classics books, mostly socialist books. I had already read some Karl Marx and with the help of a dictionary I started to understand some of the complicated words. I went on to read Tolstoy's 'War and Peace', and Dostoevsky's work including 'Crime and Punishment' whose title somewhat resonated with me at that particular time in my life. I enjoyed George Orwell. I read Malcolm Muggeridge's 'Chronicles of Wasted Time' and loved it. I was just soaking up everything I could get my hands on and the librarian was helping me to find the books I wanted and a lot of ideas were from my editions of 'The Socialist Worker'. Yes, that's right, when most of the inmates were excited about receiving their next edition of 'Playboy' or some other similar magazine, I was getting excited about the next delivery of 'The Socialist Worker'.

I had been an activist of some description for a number of years. The miners' strike was something most card carrying union members supported and would take days off work to go on the marches. There was a real sense of solidarity on these marches that sometimes involved thousands of protesters. It was the same with the anti-apartheid movement against what was happening in South Africa. I would read about the courage of Nelson Mandela and the story of Steve Beko and was so moved by their struggles.

I wasn't of much use to anyone locked up here and so I would educate myself and I made a decision that things were going to change when I got out this time. I had wasted enough of my life and I started writing letters telling everyone that I would be making a new life when I get out. I had never felt this way before, in fact up until this time I had always been adamant that I would never change.

With all my good intentions and not having anyone to meet me outside the prison gates with a handful of drugs this time, I was released and made my way home. I arrived back in Newark but all of my good intentions had a fatal flaw that I had no concept of at that time and would not learn about for some years to come, and that was that all my good intentions were of little consequence when they were faced with my addiction. When I innocently went to the pub to celebrate my release by having a few drinks with my mates, and then afterwards we would go back to someone else's house and drink a bit more and have a few spliffs, I mean where is the harm in that? What I didn't know is those few drinks and a few spliffs had woken something inside of me that had laid dormant for a couple of years and it was hungry, and the drinks and a few spliffs was not nearly enough. I might hold on to my good intentions with white knuckles and willpower but sooner or later I would find myself with my head in my hands and a full blown heroin addiction again and my hopes and dreams in tatters.

It was around this time I was introduced to someone that became a good friend. I was still of no fixed abode and floating around different peoples' houses and not long out of prison. One day, someone told me they had a friend who they were worried about. His wife had left him and as a result he had attempted to kill himself by standing in a bowl of water on the dining table and sticking his fingers in the light socket, which resulted in him being blown off the table, blowing all the fuses in the house and being held for a while in the local psychiatric ward. They thought it would be a good idea for me to move in with him to keep an eye on him!! To this day I can't fathom out why someone would think this was a good idea!? I mean, you couldn't make this stuff up. I thought it was a great idea, a new place that was safe and so my trusty red travelling trunk with my few worldly possessions in, although the album collection was increasing, had a new home for a while.

After a few drug-fuelled parties at his house, my friend soon started to forget about his marital problems and he loved the party drugs and I imagine on some days he would have had difficulty remembering his ex-wife's name. It wasn't long before he found himself a girlfriend and on one particular night they decided they wanted to do an acid trip. I was a bit apprehensive from my own experience of what can happen if it goes wrong and they have a bad trip, but it was their first time so I agreed to chaperone them and take them into town and make sure they both got home safely. In theory it sounded good and I thought I was being responsible but what actually happened is I got blind drunk and they had to carry me home.

One day, I received some devastating news. I can't remember how I was told but I found out my mum had been diagnosed with cancer. She was living with a man called Eric who had been the owner of The Bowling Green. I didn't have much time for this man and I was so angry that he was with my mum in her house so shortly after my dad had died. I had had many dealings with him and a couple of his sons over the years. One ended up with a court case after a fight with one of his sons and even though I was acquitted, I was not on the best of terms to say the least. My mum and Eric hadn't been together long when she found out about her cancer but I have to admit, that man did everything in his power to make her as comfortable as possible. He was a chef by trade and would cook wonderful meals for her, even when sometimes it was impossible for her to eat anything. My mum was being treated at home and I would go to visit her and sit next to her bed and try to allay any worries she might have about me. I didn't want her last days to be spent worrying about what I was doing and so I would try to paint a bright picture of where my life was going even though that was far from the truth.

It wouldn't be long before she was taken to hospital as she was reaching the end. One evening I was sat at her bedside, just me and her. It was in a quite big ward, all the lights were low except for perhaps one or two above a few of the beds and my mum was heavily sedated at this time and I can remember her turning her head and looking down the ward and she said to me "Can you see that little boy knelt at the side of that lady's bed?" and I said "Yes, Mum, I can". It might seem strange but in that moment I felt a connection with her because I knew the drugs she was on would cause her to hallucinate because I had experienced it using the same drugs but I also wondered if she had seen the spirit of a child comforting someone they loved in their final hours. I like to think that but I am pleased that I could allow her that moment and not interfere in what she could see. That was the last time I saw her alive. A few days later, on a

Sunday afternoon, Alan tracked me down to someone's house to say Mum had passed away that day. I knew this day would come but I wasn't prepared for it and just found it so unbearably painful. So, what do I do? I just used more drugs to try and deal with these overwhelming feelings. I don't know if I was outwardly showing how I felt but inside it was crushing. All I could feel was a mixture of loss and guilt. The guilt of not being with her at the end and the guilt of what I had put her through over the years. I didn't want these feelings and so I did my usual trick to batten down the hatches, self medicate and try to not let anything in. I was a mess and not capable of being involved in the funeral arrangements. I just left it to everyone else. Eric and Alan made the funeral arrangements and I am not sure if I was involved at all. I am sure mum would have everything in place before she passed away because she always insisted on paying her own way. She was a strong independent woman who had worked hard all her life.

I was told a story just after this about my mum's white Samoyed dog that she loved and on the day that she died the dog escaped from the house and was found sat outside the main entrance of the hospital. I am a firm believer in the ability of animals to sense things that we are incapable of but there was a part of me that thought even the dog knew where he needed to be and I as usual was missing. I had spent time with my mum while she was ill but there were so many other times when I should and could have been there but instead, laid somewhere in a drug fueled stupor.

Losing my mum was hard and the funeral came along. She would also be buried in the same plot as my brother and my dad, who had only died two years before. Although I was hurting, I was keeping it together to a certain extent. Alan and I received some money from my mum's estate and I was determined I wasn't going to squander it on drugs and drink. I made a decision that another trip to that Greek island would do me a world of good. So, myself and a couple of brothers I had known for years, Paul and Neil Campion, planned the trip together. This time we would go on the 'Magic Plane" instead of the 'Magic Bus. So, off we went with our backpacks, some hash and a few acid trips! I wasn't sure about the acid trips but being the eternal optimist, I thought it would be different this time and besides, I knew the island we were going to and they were all single-story buildings, there were no buses just donkeys so it might not be that easy to top myself this time if things go pear-shaped.

We stayed on the same beach that I had previously stayed on about three years ago and enjoyed the sun, the sand and the sea. When I did take the acid trip it was uneventful, thank goodness, and I think we spent most of the day in a shop that had bowls of coloured glass beads for making jewellery and found it fascinating to run our fingers through the multi-coloured beads and giggling like naughty children. I have no idea what the proprietor thought of us, these crazy English people.

We all enjoyed the holiday even though this time it had only been for a week or two. Unfortunately we would have to return to Newark but the upside of it was within a couple of weeks of getting back I was to meet my future and present wife, under circumstances that would not paint me in a good light but somehow I got away with it.

# 13
# THE LINEUP

Well, I no sooner arrived in Newark than I was arrested and taken in for questioning. It seems that just before I went to Greece someone had stolen some electrical items after smashing the front window of an electrical shop in the town. A witness had come forward from a hotel opposite and said they had seen someone riding a butcher's bike and loading up the basket in the front with items from the shop. Back then I owned an old multi-coloured butcher's bike, painted in Rasta colours of red, green and gold. I explained that it wasn't me (which was true) but they still wanted me to come into the police station and stand in an identity parade. I really hadn't done this but I could understand how if someone had seen the window already broken they might have been tempted to help themselves and who knows that might have happened.

The day came that I was due to go in for the lineup and I had nipped into a bar called The White Hart and as I came from the bar I saw a girl that I had previously seen briefly at my brother's house playing mahjong. I was struck by her stunning looks. I could see she was Asian and had beautiful long dark hair that reached her lower back. I was more than a little interested. So I introduced myself and mentioned that I had seen her at Alan's house a few days ago. We began chatting away and learned her name was Cindy but then it was time for me to go, and I remember her asking me where I was going and I explained about the lineup. She asked what I had in the bag I was carrying and I told her it was a sandwich and a book because I didn't know how long I would be in there, which seemed to amuse her. The lineup never happened in the end because they couldn't find eight or more local people with a suntan in December!

Going to Greece for a couple of weeks had not managed to curb my drug use by any degree, in fact it was getting worse. I had seen drug services over the years that prescribed methadone which was a substitute for heroin. It came in the form of a green liquid full of sugar to disguise its awful taste. Once a week,

I would need to travel to Nottingham to collect my weekly script that would consist of a bottle with a week's supply of this substitute drug. I was taking this on and off for about fifteen years. It was a way to stay out of prison and it was useful whenever I was working and although it was legal I couldn't divulge that I was using it because if the bosses found out and I was drug tested I would lose my job. Lucky for me they weren't as keen to drug test employees in those early days. That was fortunate for the employer also as they would most probably lose half their workforce! This was just the way things were in those days. The construction industry as I knew it was mostly about heavy drinking with the older generation but the younger ones would be using amphetamines and cannabis. Only a very few would be using opiates or injecting. It's even worse now with cocaine being so available and relatively cheap.

When I was not locked up, power station work was still my main source of income. One day, I overheard my manager saying to someone "How is it the other managers' have teams that are all 'time served' and my crew have all 'served time'?" and he was right most of them had. I could usually keep things pretty much under control while I was working and I would take my methadone in the morning and it would get me through my ten or twelve hour shift, so for a while I had some resemblance stability; well, my definition of it. When I look back it is hard to understand how I could comprehend any part of that insane life I was leading as having any form of stability or normality in it but I did. I was working every day, earning a good wage and I wasn't being chased by the police. This was as normal as I could hope for at that time.

I couldn't stop thinking about Cindy, the girl that I had recently met. I had somehow managed to talk her into coming out for a drink with me. It was our first date and I can remember how nervous I was. I had gone to great lengths to look smart and well groomed. It didn't quite go to plan. A combination of haste and nerves had caused me to cut myself shaving and a well-meaning friend had suggested putting salt on it as that would stop the bleeding, but instead made it worse. So, now I am about to meet Cindy who I really want to make a good impression on with a piece of toilet roll stuck on my face and every time I tried to remove it would start bleeding again. I was so embarrassed but Cindy seemed to see the funny side of it and still reminds me of it every now and again.

I needed to redeem myself so although we had a couple of more nights out together it was coming up to Valentine's Day that also fell on

Cindy's birthday; the perfect opportunity. My friend Kenny had a flat in town and I told him I wanted to impress someone and wanted to cook her a meal on her birthday and so he allowed me to use the flat and his kitchen. Well, the day came and it seemed as if I was in that kitchen all day but I had to pull this off.

Cindy arrived and I sat her down and congratulated her and gave her cards and flowers and then started to serve up my culinary delights. The night went really well. She told me that the meal was wonderful and she had thoroughly enjoyed it. Yes! Somehow I had pulled it off! Sometime later she told me that on that night she had wandered into the kitchen by mistake and OMG she said there were pans everywhere it looked like a bomb had gone off inside the kitchen!

I think the meal clinched it because we were going out more often now and I couldn't have been happier. Cindy was a single parent with a daughter named Theresa. Cindy and I were getting closer and one day she took me to her flat where I met Theresa for the first time. I can remember this sweet little four or five year old playing with her toys and giving me the odd glance as if trying to work out who I was and what I was doing in her house.

It wasn't long after this that I was allowed to stop the odd night. I am not sure how much

Cindy knew about me at this time and I don't think I was very open for obvious reasons but it wouldn't be long before everything was out in the open.

I had only had a couple of charges of shoplifting and a possession of cannabis charges in just over a year. It wasn't that I had quietened down, it was more of a case of good fortune and that I was buying street drugs now and not breaking into chemists. During this time I had still been visiting Steven and Jane at the foster parents' house. It was on the same estate, but this was about to come to an end when they came across the write-ups in the local paper about my drug use and so I was asked not to come to the house again and I couldn't see the children. I reluctantly agreed. I thought I was doing this for the right reasons but I was going to regret that at a later date.

Cindy and I were still seeing more of each other and I eventually moved in with her and Theresa. I was still being prescribed methadone that I would use for work mostly but my work was seasonal. I would start around March and finish in October. The repairs on power stations always took place in the summer months when the demand for electricity was at its lowest. Everyone looked forward to being made redundant at the end of the contract but I also knew that this was the time when my drug use would increase and my life would drastically go downhill. I was subsidising my unemployment benefit money at that time by doing cash-in-the hand work mostly with local scrap merchants. I would do all the repair work on their skips or any other welding and patching up that needed doing. One of these scrap merchants was called Robert Price who I had known for years. He had a reputation for getting up to all sorts that got him as much attention from the police as myself but for different reasons. I have been involved in a few of his escapades and had a few close calls and I could go on to tell you some of the crazy things that we got up to but it would take over the book.

Cindy and I had been together for a couple of years and I was trying to keep a low profile and keep out of trouble but trouble had a way of finding me.  Out of the blue, I was approached by Mick who I hadn't seen for some time and he introduced me to a guy called Bob Powell who had recently been released on 'home leave' from prison. Home leave is when you are near the end of a long sentence and the prison let an inmate out to go home for a few days and then they return to prison to finish their sentence.

This guy, Powell had got himself into a lot of debt in prison and needed money or drugs to smuggle back in and clear the debt. Someone had told him about a couple of eccentric farmer brothers that were rumoured to have a hoard of sovereigns hidden in the house. Powell and someone else had broken into this house and not found what they were looking for but stole a number of guns, mostly antique dueling pistols. I didn't have anything to do with that break in and the reason was that I didn't break into houses. I didn't have much of a code of honour as such, but I had a few things I swore I would never do and they were that I would never break into a working man's house, I would never inform on anyone to save myself and I would never hit a woman.

Things went from bad to worse and I was about to find myself looking at a long sentence. A chemist was broken into and I was implicated in it. Powell had not returned to prison and had gone on the run and now the police had found out he was hiding in Newark and were searching for him. I didn't know this at the time but on the night of the guns being taken there was an attempted armed hold-up on a local supermarket; it seems one of the guns was a 45 revolver. To this day, I wonder if Powell held that supermarket up because it is a bit of a coincidence to say the least that it happened the same night. Anyway, he took it to his grave as he died a few years later.

It was time to make a move and Cindy asked someone to look after Theresa for a few days while this blew over and we went to stay at my friend's house who was on holiday in Spain at the time. We were told that armed police had been outside Cindy's flat and they were searching for me.

I had some drugs with me and we had food and we just stayed in the house until I could work something out but after a couple of days a police car pulled up outside the house and who should be sat in the back of it but my so-called friend, Mick. The house was clean (no drugs) and they came in and arrested me.

I was taken back to the police station and questioned for hours but just refused to answer their questions. I had been accused of handling stolen firearms that included a class one firearm and I was accused of breaking into a chemist. This was serious because I was in breach of the Firearms Act, which prohibits me from possessing a firearm for five years after my last sentence, which had only been two years before.

The first hurdle I needed to get over was that I was to be put in a lineup for the attempted armed robbery on the supermarket. I knew that I hadn't been anywhere near it but I was convinced the police would set me up or the witness felt obliged to pick someone out and it was bound to be me! Anyway, all my fears were unfounded and it was over and I could breathe again.

I had three co-accused: Powell, Mick and a driver. Both Powell and Mick had made statements implicating me as the person who broke into the chemist and as much as the police tried to force me to admit that I was there I strenuously denied it. After forty-eight hours they had to charge release or me me and I was charged and taken before the magistrates with the others and remanded to Lincoln Prison. At this time, Powell had been returned to prison to continue his unspent sentence. Mick and I were remanded and the driver (also called Mick) was bailed.

We were well known by now with the prison officers in the reception area where we were processed into the remand wing. It could take up to a couple of hours. In the reception area they had two or three cells that were segregated for Rule 43s; these were either sex offenders or someone who had enemies in the prison. Some of the officers knew how we felt about paedophiles and sex offenders and if any were being held as we were being processed they would tell us what they had done, leave their door unlocked and turn a blind eye as we went in and beat the shit out of them. This happened quite often because we would be coming through every week for months. The reason for that was at that time we couldn't be remanded for more than seven days. So, every week we would make the trip back to Newark where I would be questioned, pressured, threatened and beaten. It was a relief when it was time to go back to the prison. Cindy would be allowed to visit me in the police cell and bring me clean clothes and they even tried to put pressure on her to get me to admit to the charges.

I never made a complaint about the beatings in the police cells. It was as if acknowledging it would somehow have them think they bothered me in the slightest and they didn't. Some of these detectives would go to any lengths to secure a conviction and especially when they had someone like me that they had a serious problem with. I had gone out of my way to do things to humiliate them in the past so it was only fair they had a chance to get their own back but it was about me and them. Cindy wasn't part of this but I couldn't protect her.

The beatings were becoming more intense as we got closer to a trial date. I wouldn't give them the satisfaction of thinking I gave a toss by making a complaint about my treatment but it was taken out of my hands because when we returned to the reception at Lincoln, everyone is searched and that meant stripping off naked and turning around in a full circle and so the guards were noticing these bruises I was coming back with and started asking me about them. I don't know what excuse I made but from that day they began listing on a sheet that had a print out of the outline of a body, front and back, and they would circle areas where I had a bruise and then check it when I came back. I think at some point during questioning at Newark I might have inadvertently let this information slip out and they seemed to suddenly lose interest in the physical aspect of their questioning techniques.

Back in prison, I was to meet my solicitor and after a while I would receive a copy of the depositions for the case so now I could see everything they had said and nothing surprised until I read a statement one of the detectives had made saying I had admitted part of it. I knew they were desperate and I wanted to confront them about it. I had a chance at the magistrates hearing before the case was sent to crown court. The officer involved was in court with the others and I stood up at some point and said "If this officer is prepared to stand by what he has said about me in his statement then it means he is prepared to commit perjury to try and convict me".

My solicitor at the time was a lady and her name was Susan. She explained to me that at trial we couldn't call the detective a liar in court even if he was, and that my job was to go back to my cell in Lincoln and go through those depositions with a fine-toothed comb and highlight the relevant areas and put "misinterpretation of answer" as this would be the areas that were closer to the truth without calling him an outright liar. I wasn't happy about it but I did it and I spent every spare moment studying them before the trial.

Also while I was waiting for the trial, there was an outbreak of salmonella poisoning in the prison and I had petitioned the governor to eat my own food until it was over but he refused, so I went on hunger strike and was put down the punishment block in a single cell with cardboard furniture and a mattress on the floor. Three times a day they would plate meals up for me and weigh them before putting them in the cell and an hour or so later they would collect the plate, weigh it to check if I had eaten anything and then dispose of it. This went on for ten days until Cindy went on Radio Lincoln and said what was happening. Then, I was suddenly put back into my original cell. I didn't achieve anything but it was another case of not giving in no matter what and sticking two fingers up at them!

During this time I had been in the same cell as Mick and although that was strained to say the least, I didn't confront him about seeing him in the car with the police when they picked me up. I was working on the old saying of 'keeping your friends close and your enemies closer'. I didn't think Mick had the guts to go 'Queen's Evidence' against me to try to get a lighter sentence but I didn't want to give him an excuse, so I kept quiet. Powell was a different story and a worry to me right up until the trial.

Mick and Powell pleaded guilty and were sentenced before my trial and both received five-year sentences. One good thing that came out of that was the judge had classed the guns as antiques and so they didn't come under the Firearms Act, so that was a potential five year sentence that I didn't need to worry about. I had seen Mick briefly before he was moved to another prison and he told me that his solicitor had said that I had no chance of a not guilty plea and would end up with a minimum of seven years.

It came to the fateful day and I had two charges; the first was burglary of a chemist and the second of handling stolen goods, the guns. I was advised to plead guilty to the lesser charge and concentrate on the main charge. I reluctantly agreed and the trial commenced. I don't think many people could stand in the dock of a crown court and not be intimidated by the sombre atmosphere and the judge and barristers in their wigs and gowns. I can remember every moment as if it was yesterday. I was taken out of the cell and a set of steep stairs take you straight up into the dock and you are met with all this hustle and bustle, sifting through paperwork, a glance from my barrister and an encouraging smile; my heart is in my mouth. The judge enters and everyone stands and is asked to be silent.

And now it begins. I give my name and sit down. The detectives give their evidence one at a time. At one point, the barrister asks the detective who had lied in his statement if when he arrested me did he know I was guilty and he answers "Yes" and the Barrister went on to ask "How did you know?" At this point he is stumped and stammering, because he thought I was guilty because he had seen the statements Frizzel and Powell had made against me but he isn't allowed to mention them. This was a turning point for me and just deserts for the detective that lied about me.

The jury went out and I was taken down to the cells to await the verdict. It was the longest wait of my life but it was only for about an hour. I was taken back up into the dock and I saw Cindy in the public gallery and gave her a smile as the judge entered. I knew if this went the wrong way I was going to prison for a long time and it was different this time, I actually had someone who cared about me and I cared about her. I daren't say 'love' just in case it all went wrong and I would have to say goodbye to her.

The jury came in and read out the verdict, "NOT GUILTY". I was so ecstatic, I hardly heard the judge sentencing me to twelve months imprisonment for handling the guns. My time spent on remand would count against that sentence leaving me with about three months to do. I got a chance to see Cindy before 'they' took me back to Prison. I might have been the happiest inmate in that prison that night.

# 14
## CHAOS WAS ON ITS WAY

The next morning I was counting my blessings and making plans for when I would be released. I was never a trusting person and always expected something to go wrong. It wasn't unusual for people to get what is known as a 'gate arrest'. This is where the police find out about a new offence and will arrest people as they are about to be released from prison. I knew that I had offences that I had got away with so it was always a possibility.

Mick was a Jekyll and Hyde character and when he wasn't using drugs he was a pleasure to be around, funny, a bit of a ladies man with his long black hair and moustache. He was a good friend, but when he was using drugs he would completely change. I knew early on in our time together that once he was arrested he would do whatever he could to get out. I expected him to grass me up but I didn't see it as a problem at the time. It just made me more vigilant and careful. As long as they didn't find evidence against me, what he said didn't matter. After I left prison Mick and I were to part company and I kept him at arm's length. In fact he left Newark and moved to Lincoln shortly after being released.

Figure 6 - Cindy & Theresa

While I was finishing this particular sentence I was making plans for the future; this was my wake-up call and I was determined not to waste it. Cindy had been solid throughout this time and she deserved better than this. I made a decision to make some real changes in my life. I had a good trade and could provide for her and her daughter, Theresa. I was determined and so sure I could do this. I was writing letters every day to Cindy telling her what I intended to do and promising that things would be different.

It wouldn't be long before my release day arrived and I had decided that I was going to turn my life around and put all this behind me. This had been a close call and I could have been locked up for a lot longer. I would start this new life by proposing to Cindy! We had been talking about this in our letters and on visits and so when I did ask her officially she agreed and we were married a few weeks later. We had the most inexpensive wedding of all and it cost us a total of around £50! It was January 1984. After the registry office, we had a reception above a local public bar. Everyone brought food with them. Eric, my mum's partner, brought a whole salmon that without doubt was the centre piece in comparison with our mostly sausage rolls, sandwiches and cakes, although we did have a wedding cake. Cindy had brought two Christmas cakes and a friend of ours iced and decorated them for us.

It was a good day with music and friends; even my mum's sister Celia came along. We both remember my friend Pat Ginnely doing his rendition of "Delaney's Donkey" (that went down a treat) and doing cartwheels on the dance floor. It was snowing that day and we all went outside to have a group photo and when we saw a copy later everyone seemed to think it looked more like a police line-up. I must say there were a few scoundrels there that day. They had a collection between them and booked us a night in a hotel not far from the reception and so that was our honeymoon night.

Figure 7 - Doddie, Cindy & Trevor

We were so happy. I knew Cindy was a special person and I had promised that things would be different this time. I was looking forward to showing my new wife that I was a man of my word, but I didn't keep it. It would always start the same way. A few drinks, a few joints and then a little bit of something else. I don't know how many times I had said to myself, "What if I just used at weekends?" but this is something I had tried and failed at for years. The 'weekends' just got longer until it was every day so why would I think it would be any different this time around? That definition of insanity comes to mind, of doing the same things over and over and expecting a different result. It would take another twelve years before I would find the answer to why I kept going back. With all the will in the world, I was fighting a battle I would always lose, with the prophecy of my dad ringing in my ears.

I am not sure how quickly my addiction progressed but we seemed to be pretty settled and happy for a while and then in November of the same year (1984) our daughter, Simone was born. Our first child together! I was so happy and proud as I held Simone in my arms and looked down into her beautiful innocent face. Theresa was seven years old and now she had a little sister. We were building our family but I was living this double life and hiding as much as I could from Cindy. Deception was an integral part of trying to hold things together. It would be an old pattern of mine where I would be working on a power station for six or seven months and I would be earning a good wage. Then the winter would come and I would have to sign on the dole and do little cash-in-the-hand jobs to get by. This is when I would supplement my income with drug deals and working for the local scrap dealers.

During these times I would spend a lot of time in Scunthorpe where I bought backstreet amphetamine powder in bulk. Scunthorpe had large amounts of addicts and it was about this time that HIV raised its ugly head. Most addicts including me were now injecting their drugs, and syringes and needles were not readily available at that time. We had to make do with what we had and that would mean washing them out after use for the next person. It was like playing Russian roulette and unfortunately most of the addicts I knew at that time and some of their partners all died after becoming HIV positive. I don't remember how many, but it was twenty plus. Some were only young kids in their late teens.

Our married life wasn't always bad. We would go swimming with the kids and go on camping holidays to Skegness where I would teach the children how to fish when they were old enough. This was still early on, they were only little so they would lay on the wooden jetty and use a fishing float as a rod with a tiny hook and line and catch minnows to put in a jar. They loved it. Later we would go into

Skegness and visit the amusements and visit the pier to buy knickerbocker glories that were so big they had to kneel on the chairs to reach the top.

I decided to take up my hunting pastime again and acquired a couple of running dogs called Fly and Ben. I remember the day we got Fly; we were on our way to a Lurcher show in Oakham with our friends Steve and Ruth. Just before we got there, our car broke down. It had a puncture and we had no spare so I rang the guy who sold me the car and he brought a spare out to us. In the meantime some bikers had stopped to see if they could help but couldn't and offered to give the girls a lift to the show. At the time Cindy was heavily pregnant with Simone and decided to take them up on their offer. It seemed a bit weird to see my pregnant wife disappearing into the distance on the back of this Hells Angel's chopper bike! Would I see her again?!

Anyway, all went well and I arrived at the Lurcher show to find Cindy hiding something under her coat. When she showed me what she had it was this beautiful little tan and white Lurcher pup. Lurchers are running dogs, that is they chase things such as rabbits and hares and they are crossed using greyhounds and other breeds. We named him Fly. Fly was greyhound and collie cross, a combination of speed and brains. He was a good dog and a faithful companion and I had him for a number of years. Ben I picked up later from a friend whose marriage had broken down and he had nowhere to keep the dog. Ben was a deerhound cross greyhound and was built for speed and endurance and, with the ferrets, I had my team. I would try to get out as often as I could. Fortunately for me I was off in the winter months, which was the hunting season and so it was a welcome distraction from my other life.

The next addition to our family was Jack, named after my dad. He arrived in 1987 on Cindy's birthday, which was also Valentine's Day. I wasn't likely to forget these birthdays. I was over the moon that we had a boy to add to our family and it felt complete. I now had two daughters and a son. I so wanted to do all the things I had missed out on with my first children. I didn't know it then but I was incapable of giving any of my kids what they really needed while I was basically drugged up all the time. I tried to pretend that it wasn't that bad, but it was.

Not long after Jack was born I have a memory that still haunts me. On this one particular day I needed to travel to Scunthorpe to pick my drugs up. I knew the police were aware of my frequent trips and were keeping an eye out for me, so I had been changing my route back to avoid them but this time I did something I would never have considered before and that was to put my family at risk. I thought I had some sort of code, principles that I would never break and here I was breaking a cardinal rule to involve my family in any of this.

I talked Cindy into coming with me with the children. I was using them to make it look like a family outing and would have told Cindy a pack of lies to get her to agree. Everything went ok and we were on our way home as we reached the outskirts of Newark and on a back country lane I saw a police dog handler's van parked facing me and as I passed him he spun around and gave chase. I panicked and could only think of getting away, I was driving as fast as I could with Cindy and my two small children strapped in their car seats at the back. Simone was around three and Jack was only about a year old. I had three of the four most important people in my life in that car and I was driving like a lunatic. The worst part was that I reached a crossroads where a main road crossed my path and I drove straight across it. I could easily have killed all of us. Cindy was screaming at me to stop, the children were crying and I carried on around a corner pulled into a farm gateway and ran off leaving my distraught family in the car.

The police officer had been joined by a motorcyclist who I found out later was an off-duty prison officer who had joined the chase. It was winter and there was some snow on the field. I threw the bag of drugs as far as I could and headed towards a farm house that was a couple of hundred yards away but the police dog had been let loose and it soon brought me down and I was arrested.

Back at the station the policemen were panicking because they couldn't find the drugs and after strip searching me and then searching the car, they went on to search Cindy and even the baby's nappy. I was so angry with them for subjecting my family to that, and I was so humiliated and ashamed at what I had just put my family through and the risk I had taken with their precious lives just to save my own skin. The thing that brought it home for me was they did find the drugs eventually and it wasn't a large quantity. I was charged with possession of amphetamine, a class B drug and when it came to court I was given a two year conditional discharge! What had I become? I had become one of the low lives I despised that had no scruples who would rob, cheat and steal from anyone to get what they wanted and they didn't care who they hurt and never did a day's work in their lives. I always thought of myself as not like most of the addicts. I always believed that there would be certain things I would never do but this had shown me that I was just like them and I hated myself for it.

I had done things I swore I would never do, no matter what and now I had done this. I had always ensured that I was the one that faced the music when I fucked up and now I felt I had committed an unforgivable betrayal. I didn't recognise the person I was becoming.

This was 1988 and I had also been involved in credit card fraud. I would buy stolen credit cards and then go into supermarkets and fill the trolley up with expensive booze and things without it looking too suspicious and forging the signature and then selling it on at half price. I got away with it for quite a while unfortunately there was more than just me doing it and someone got caught and informed on the rest of us. I was charged with numerous counts of forgery and received a fourteen-month prison sentence. This was to be my final criminal charge and I never went to court again but it wasn't the end of my criminal activities.

When I came out of that sentence I swore I was not going to prison again. For one thing I had been in a dormitory with a bunch of younger lads and It was harder for me to hold my own in there and there was always some young buck that wanted to try his luck and test me out. The other thing was deep down I wanted to be a husband and father that my family could be proud of. When the drugs were out of my system I believed all this was possible and I sincerely wanted it so much. I had been here a number of times and always failed. I wondered if I would ever make it or if there was something wrong with me. I remembered times when I took drugs for fun, parties, all-nighters, and clubs and was off to work on Monday morning.

I was still managing to go to work somehow but it had been a long time since my drug taking had been fun; those days had long gone. Now it was a matter of maintenance. I was just able to function, making life just bearable most of the time. I went back to my methadone script now I was out of prison and I wouldn't be swapping it for drugs this time, as I had in the past. Methadone had become a currency in the drug world. This time I was going to use it to get to work and hopefully stabilise myself and get back on track. Well, that was the plan!

What really happened was… I moved away from amphetamines and I had been using heroin more and more over the years. Towards the end of my chemist breaking days we came across a book in the pharmacy called a MIMS. This was a book that listed all the drugs in the pharmacy by categories and there came a time towards the end of my using days that the only category I was interested in was the analgesic list, the painkillers. Some that I found and I was now using I had never heard of. Injecting something that you didn't know the dosage or how safe it was is insanity but that never stopped me.

I was about to come to a stable period in my life where I would find myself a couple of years work. This was the time when coal fired power stations were being pressured into cutting their omissions and so they began building Fuel Gas Desulphurisation plants (F.G.D.) The one I was to work on was Ratcliffe-on-Soar power station near Nottingham. A lot of the men working there were people I knew and had worked with before many from Newark. This job would be continuous work for a little over two years. It had been a long time since I had been in continuous employment where I could book holidays in the summer. Usually summer was the busy shutdown season for me and taking time off for any reason was not tolerated. Anyone who tried was classed as a bad timekeeper and would soon find themselves without a job, so this was a welcome change for me. The work was a massive project and involved more technical work than I was used to. For instance we had to be trained up to use theodolites and dumpy levels, which was well out of my comfort zone but I soon learned to use them.

This was a better time for us as a family and although I was using occasionally it was mostly cannabis. We were at last doing normal family things like trips to the coast, camping and fishing. We had travelled a few times to Cornwall to a little fishing village called Polperro. It was beautiful and my son Steven and his wife Rachel had made the trip with us on a previous occasion but this time it was with my brother and his family that consisted of his wife Sarah and two boys George and Henry who were only small at the time. It was good to spend some time with Alan as we had drifted apart over the years. He didn't know it at the time but he was to play a pivotal role in reclaiming my life some years later.

These happy times in our lives were too short lived and they would eventually come to an end as I would need to return to Newark and then the pattern that had followed me throughout my life was about to repeat itself again. Whenever I had a stable period in my life it would be closely followed by a period of chaos and that chaos was on its way again now. All the trust I had built up over the previous couple of years was going to be destroyed in a matter of weeks or months.

After I was made redundant and I was left to my own devices, I had all this time on my hands and no structure to follow, I soon found myself back at my dealer's door buying heroin. It wasn't long before I had a habit again. We were now living in a three bedroomed council house in a cul-de-sac and I was getting involved with some heavy criminals that were visiting me at the house. I was a sort of middle-man, arranging deals for them. Cindy didn't know who they were and what they did, thank goodness. They would usually come in the early hours of the morning and be gone by the time she woke up.

The police must have become suspicious. I had a neighbour opposite me that was far too nosey and I had had a couple of altercations with him so there was no love lost between us. On one particular day, another neighbour came to tell me he had seen a camera filming my house from this person's bedroom window. It seems he had allowed the police to use his house to keep me under surveillance. I confronted him about it, that was all I could do at that time and it stopped but I was a lot more careful after that and stopped people coming to the house.

I was reaching a point where I really couldn't do this any longer and desperately wanted to stop but in the past the only way I had

195

stopped everything was when I had been locked up and I didn't want to go down that road again. I can remember at some point asking my drug worker that there must be something else, a different way, because this isn't working for me. I had been on and off methadone for over ten years and yes, it had helped me stay out of prison but it was just another drug and I was sick of it. I had heard it called 'liquid handcuffs' and that is exactly what it was. Not only did I need to take it every day but I had to be at a clinic in Nottingham once a week to collect it. I had to make special arrangements when I was working or if I needed to go out of town for any reason, even holidays were a problem as I couldn't go without it.

What a shit life I had created for myself. I was at my lowest point, at my wits' end. I had a beautiful wife and family that loved me and yet a little bag of brown powder had all this power over me. I was feeling powerlessness before I knew what it really meant. It would take me another two years of pain and suffering for me and my family before I found the start of a journey that would transform my life beyond recognition and save my marriage that was on the brink of being lost forever.

I was trying to stop now and I had told a using friend in Nottingham that I was trying to detox myself and I had reduced my methadone down to about five milligrams from fifty but I couldn't let go of that last bit. My heroin use had been reduced too and I had told my friend that I needed a place to finish my detox off. I had done plenty of cold turkey detoxes in police cells over the years to know what to expect and I didn't want my wife and kids to witness this so he offered to let me use a flat he wasn't using and gave me a key and told me I could use it any time. I think I had that key for well over a year and could never find the right day to do it, tomorrow always seemed to be a better day and so I would just carry on trying to keep my usage down to a minimum but it wasn't very consistent and I would have the odd binge and go back to reducing again. It was a perpetual cycle of nearly getting there and then starting again. It was torture.

I was offered a chance of a job in Holland around this time and I decided to take it and to do my detox there. I thought being in Newark was the problem but I was the problem. I must say, this wasn't one of my better plans! Well, the first thing is that I definitely was not in my right mind but I was desperate to get off drugs at all costs. I was going to some petrochemical plant in the middle of nowhere, what could go wrong?!

A few of us went from Newark and we all knew each other. We arrived and we were staying on a caravan park and were assigned our caravans with two people sharing, I was with my mate Billy and so we shared and moved our bags in. We then went to the site club where we were told about the job. We were also given a cost of living allowance that was paid in cash. It was about £200 so it was enough to live on.

I had brought some tablets that would help my withdrawal symptoms, they were DF118s also known as Dihydrocodeine. I was hoping they wouldn't be too severe as I had been reducing recently. I also left my bank cards with Cindy so I didn't get tempted to do anything stupid. It was our first night and so off to the club for a few beers and back to the caravan ready for work the next morning. I can remember ringing Cindy every night after the pub and telling her how well I was doing. I was starting to believe in myself and that my harebrained plan just might work.

This was short lived because after a few days the lads were soon smoking dope in the caravans and, what with the drink involved, it wasn't long before the beast within me was woken up and I was looking for something stronger to tame it. I had found that Rotterdam was only an hour away on the train

and I was off to find some heroin. I
befriended a couple of homeless young lads
that would find what I wanted and I would
give them a bit and make my way back to the
caravan park. It worked pretty well until one
night as I was doing a deal someone snatched
my money and ran off. I ran after him. He
looked like he was living on the streets. I
caught up with him and he pulled a small knife
on me but I soon had him on the ground and
as I was trying to get my money out of his
pockets a crowd was gathering and people
were shouting at me out of windows and it
was getting a bit hairy. I managed to get most
of my money and made a hasty retreat. The
two homeless guys had hung around and
helped me and we went and finished our
business. It wasn't until later that I realised
how dangerous that situation had been.

I had started asking Cindy to send me extra
money and I think she suspected that I might
be using again. I suggested she come over for
a weekend and she did. We went to
Amsterdam for a day. I was snorting cocaine
in the toilets behind Cindy's back for that
weekend. Billy let us have the caravan to
ourselves. Cindy knew all the lads I worked
with and cooked us all a big curry before she
left which was well appreciated as none of us
were very good cooks.

I don't know what happened- I wonder if Cindy coming over had made everyone homesick- but we had made a pact before we left Newark that if we left we would all leave together and the following day that is just what happened. We all packed our bags and left for the airport and I arrived home not long after Cindy.

Next I would get a phone call off my brother that was going to change everything. He was about to play his pivotal part in the story...

# 15
## THE PHONE CALL

We are back from Holland and my heroin addiction is escalating. So much for my bright idea of getting clean over there. I always blamed being in Newark for my problems but it didn't matter where I went. It was me that was the problem and one day I would find the reason why.

My family life is going down the drain fast. One of the last Christmases before I found help was particularly horrendous. For the last four or five years, I would visit my dealer in Edwinstowe, a small village about ten miles away from Newark. The dealer lived with his elderly mother who was at that time bedridden and very rarely left her ground-floor bedroom while he did his business from the front room.

Every Christmas Eve, I would be at his house collecting enough drugs to last me until Boxing Day and his last words to me before I left were "Don't come around on Christmas Day because I won't serve you" and I would agree but every Christmas Day I was on his doorstep banging on the door having used it all and refusing to leave until he sorted me out. He would be as angry as hell but he knew I wasn't going anywhere until I got what I came for.

Figure 8 - Trevor & Alan

This particular Christmas morning I had woken to the sounds of my children excitedly opening their presents. I was withdrawing and feeling terrible, all I could think of was getting to Edwinstowe and getting some more drugs. I told Cindy I had to nip out and she was so angry with me and said, "You could at least stay long enough to see the children open their presents". I remember clearly sitting watching their happy faces ripping open their presents and the sheer joy on their faces when they found a toy or something else inside. Cindy had organised all this. I hadn't done anything besides earn a bit of money to pay for them. I hated that I was thinking, "For Christ sake just hurry up, I need to go", and then seeing the disappointment in their faces as I left the house and promised not to be long but I knew this was a lie and I would most probably not make Christmas dinner. I hated myself. I knew this was not who I really was, I knew this wasn't my true nature but I felt powerless, everything I did revolved around this small bag of powder. I felt like a complete loser and the drugs might help with the physical withdrawals but it wouldn't take away how I felt about myself.

The second and last time I remember is the same sort of scenario only on Boxing Day. My car broke down on the way back from Edwinstowe and I had to leave it in Newark somewhere. I arrived home late for dinner and by this time I had added crack cocaine to my rapidly declining life of drugs. In an ironic way I think it was a blessing in disguise because it destroyed any last remnants of my belief that I had any control over my addiction. Crack cocaine had chewed me up and spat me out and I knew it. I had managed to get a home detox kit before the Christmas break and decided to try and detox myself, so on the Boxing Day morning I bit the bullet and began the process. I managed to last until that evening and then decided that I just couldn't do it. There was no way that the detox kit was going to hold me and the withdrawal had become too painful, and so I jumped in another car that I was getting ready for the road. Even though it had no tax or MOT and it wasn't very roadworthy, this would not stop me. Once the obsession had taken over me, wild horses couldn't stop me.

The home detox included sedatives and I had taken them all, I was having trouble focusing and everything on the road was a blur. I must have been weaving about and was having trouble keeping my eyes open, and then as I came around a bend on the outskirts of

Newark I clipped a car's wing mirror coming in the opposite direction. I then lost control altogether and went through some trees snapping off two concrete posts, and nearly hit a man taking his dog for a walk. The car was completely wrecked. I wasn't injured but now the only thing I was concerned about was "How the Hell am I going to get to my dealer now?" People came out of their houses asking if I was ok and fussing about but I just wanted to get away. The guy that I had clipped and knocked his wing mirror off had doubled back and was asking me what happened. It was winter and there was a bit of snow and ice still about so I blamed that. I found out he was a police officer on his way to work; what about that for bad luck? The police soon arrived and questioned me and breathalysed me and took my details and that was it. I can't remember being searched or any questions about drugs but I do remember telling a story to the policeman that I was on my way to meet my wife who would be waiting for me in a public house in Edwinstowe. The traffic division's police base at that time was in Edwinstowe and I had an idea he might be heading that way and I was right. I relaxed when he agreed to drop me off. It didn't occur to me that I had no idea how I was going to get home. This was the tunnel vision that I had become so accustomed to, together with the lies that seemed to just roll off my tongue with ease, all that mattered was getting that little bag of brown powder or that small white rock of crack cocaine, that would give me temporary relief from this pain but it was always short-lived. The guilt and shame of what I was putting my family through would creep back in and settle like a lead ball in the pit of my stomach every time, but I couldn't stop. I was that same Jekyll and Hyde character that I had described Mick as being.

I despised myself and all those I was associating with. I always thought I was different, not like the rest of them but now here I was just another low-life junkie. I was beaten and I had never admitted that to myself. I had never relied on anyone for what I wanted and here I was catching the crumbs off this dealer's table and having to tolerate his minions that scuttled around blowing smoke up his arse and being at his beck and call for a few more crumbs. I was hooked and trapped and now crack cocaine had become part of the equation and sealed my fate. My downward spiral was accelerating and I had no brakes to slow it down.

For about the last year of my using, I was a physical and mental mess. I was still using the Methadone script to get to work when I got the call to start another contract, but I was virtually dragging myself there, luckily I had friends that knew I had a drug problem and covered for me on the bad days that were now getting more frequent. After finishing my ten or sometimes twelve-hour shifts in a hot and dusty environment I would go straight to Edwinstowe and use crack and heroin until the early hours and the drive home and sleep on the settee and get up for work at 6am and then do it all over again. I stopped washing myself. I would change my clothes occasionally and I was living on something called Muller Rice, a tub of rice pudding with a bit of jam in the bottom. It was easy to digest. Cindy and I were hardly speaking but I had this crazy idea that as long as I went to work things were not that bad. It was my drowning man's straw to cling onto. In all the years of my using I could never remember getting in the state I found myself now. Even my workmates were concerned for me and had picked up on my lack of personal hygiene and I was nicknamed "Polecat" which I was not over the moon about to say the least but it was well deserved.

This was a far cry from those early days as a Mod where everything was about appearances. I loved getting ready for a night out, showered, shaved and aftershave on. All my clothes laid out on the bed washed and ironed, a handful of pills and the excitement of a night out with my friends. This was a distant memory that was now lost forever.

I was in 100% survival mode now and I managed to get through that contract and the following winter. It was during those winter months that I would still take my dogs, Fly and Ben out for a run. Mostly it would be in the dead of night with a lamp to try and catch a couple of rabbits. I was becoming more of a recluse and not wanting to see anyone or anyone to see me. The moonless nights far from houses or roads was where I would find some sense of solace. One night in particular, is so clear to me... I had walked for a few miles and came into a field that was pitch dark and I walked to the centre of the field and curled up in a ball and I just wanted it to all go away and I think I prayed for the first time in a long time; it was short and sweet, just "Somebody, please help me. I am so tired of this and I can't go on anymore". I bathed in that darkness for a little while with my dogs around me, they sensed my pain and they nuzzled my tear-stained face and then curled up each side of me and I felt safe for a moment but eventually I had to get up with my wet and muddy knees and go home. I had been in fields like this before feeling the same way but this night was different, I was broken and for me to pray to a God I didn't believe in proved it and I guess this is why it has stayed with me.

Cindy and I were at breaking point too but a number of synchronicities were about to happen that would change the course of my life forever and save me and our marriage. This next part of my story is about hope and infinite possibilities in spite of where my life had taken me where I found myself at this point, how far down the scale I might have slipped, there is always HOPE.

I was still looking at ways to escape my personal nightmare, this black hole I found myself in that had no walls. I didn't have the courage to just stop and go "cold turkey." The thought of it put the fear of God into me. I can remember how painful it was when I had been locked in police cells and left to go through the withdrawal. At one time a heroin detox was three bad days and then things would start to improve but withdrawal from Methadone was a lot harder and it feels as if it had got into your very bones, every part of my body ached, hot and cold sweats, vomiting and desperate trips to the toilet. I needed help and I told my drug worker again that I wanted to detox and there must be something he can do to help me and he came back to me the following week and said "I can offer you a few days in a psychiatric unit" and I agreed without hesitation. Thankfully I wouldn't need to take up his offer because something else was about to come my way from an unexpected source. This was the first of many synchronicities that were about to fall into place. This is where I believe some kind of divine intervention was taking place; could it be coming about from that pitiful prayer I made in the middle of a field in the dead of night with my dogs? Could this be true?

Out of the blue one day, I had a phone call from my brother who I hadn't spoken to for quite some time and he asked me if there was a way for me to go into treatment for my addiction would I be up for it. I said 'Yes, of course' and he said that he would make some enquiries. He had known someone who had been into an addiction clinic in Nottingham and was going to make some enquiries on my behalf. I was excited, frightened and convinced I was going to be disappointed.

Maybe I ought to have had more faith in the prayer I offered on that night with my dogs. The first hurdle was when I got a phone call a few days later from a lady that was going to try and get me the funding I needed through my doctor. The doctor was Dr Robertson and he agreed to the funding. The lady that secured this funding was called Benta and I was ecstatic when she told me the news. I now had to wait for a bed to come available that could be up to three months. I didn't know it at the time but my brother Alan was doing a lot of work behind the scenes to make this happen. Something else I was unaware of, was that it was Cindy that had gone to Alan and asked for his help in the first place.

While I was waiting I had a call to start work and I was one of the first people on the site so it was going to be for quite a few weeks and already I was working out how I could put the treatment off until after the contract finished. I didn't have to worry though, whoever was answering my prayer knew how stupid I could be and would have to make it a no-brainer for this poor fool! A few days later I was doing a run to pick up some crack for the dealer. It was dark and I broke down on a bend. I was on my own and needed to get the car off the road before it caused an accident so I proceeded to put my back against the back of the car and push it off the road and just as I got it onto the verge my foot slipped and I just felt this excruciating pain shoot up the back of my leg and I instantly knew it was more than a strain. I'm not sure what happened next but someone did come out to me and get the car going and I carried on into Nottingham, on the way I picked a couple of crepe bandages up and tried wrapped it tightly around my calf. It helped a little bit but the pain was terrible. I did what I needed to do and got back to Edwinstowe with the drugs, smoked some crack, had another hit (injection) of heroin and made my way home.

I was supposed to be at work the next morning but I woke up during the night with pain like I had never experienced before. I had no choice but to go to the hospital. I arrived at A&E and was taken for an X-ray where I was told I had ruptured my Achilles tendon and had to have my leg in plaster. All I could think was this is the worst thing that could happen to me and how much money I was going to lose. What I didn't realise is that this was the best thing that could have happened and it wasn't until later that I thought it might be some kind of divine intervention.

I left the hospital with a full plaster, struggling to use the crutches and also feeling very sorry for myself. I went home sulking like a kid and plonked myself in a chair, all I could think about was what I had lost and not for one second did I see it as a God-given opportunity.

I also had other considerations, I still had a habit that needed feeding and how the Hell was I going to get my drugs? I don't know if it was that day or the next day but I worked out if I moved the driver's seat as far back as possible I could use the pedals in the car and drive in a fashion. It was so dangerous and as much as I didn't trust anyone there came a point where I had to get someone to go for me.

This only went on for a few days because whoever was watching over me had everything covered. One morning only a few days after my accident, I was sitting at home waiting for my drugs to be delivered when I received a phone call from Benta at the Nottingham Clinic saying that she had some good news and some bad news for me. Fearing the worst I asked for the good news first and she told me they had a bed for me, my heart was racing. So what was the bad news then? She said I had to come in tomorrow". I blurted out "Thank you so much and that is not bad news, believe me". I was told I needed to be at the main reception at two o'clock the next day and not to be late. After the phone call, all I could do was burst into tears. The sheer relief that I had been given this chance. I knew deep down that I wouldn't get another chance like this, that this was it for me, "do or die" and meant that literally.

I rang Cindy straight away and told her the good news but she was far from impressed and I can't blame her. She heard me countless times make empty promises that always ended in disappointment for her. I knew this was going to be different but words are cheap and I knew I was going to have to prove it. I knew that it wasn't going to be easy and I didn't know for sure if we would make it and she told me later she felt the same way.

I arranged for someone to drive me there the next day but I went via Edwinstowe and had my last use up of drugs before I went to the clinic. The last piece that was needed and fell into place was when I was told that the treatment was for six weeks, I had just been given a sick note which was written up for six weeks for my injury, so my employers didn't need to know where I was. Everything was in place, now it was up to me.

# 16
## MY LAST CHANCE

I am in the door and I am scared but would never admit it. Someone asks, "How are you?" and I answer "Good" with a smile. This is something I have always been able to do for as long as I can remember, even if I felt I was dying and broken on the inside. I was sitting there in the reception area and everything inside of me was saying 'run!' The door was in my view to the right and my natural instinct when frightened was to fight or escape as fast as I could from whatever scared me. I needed to get away from the front door; it was too close. I felt this time my survival instinct might well sabotage what I believed was my last chance to find a way out of this living nightmare I had created. I don't know that I would've managed to get very far on my crutches but I was called into the office. I sat down to answer a list of questions and was relieved to not be left on my own. The questions were a welcomed distraction from my thoughts and I began to relax a little. I remember one of the questions was about my drug use and how much I was using a day and I can remember lying about this and played it down saying I used less. I couldn't understand why I would do that. If I had been after a script off my drug worker I would be doing the opposite and exaggerating how much I was using.

I was determined to do this and deep down I knew it was going to take every resource I had. I was going to do whatever it took and under no circumstances was I going anywhere, no matter what! I had been running all my life; I needed to find the courage to stop, turn around and face up to what was in front of me.

I was eventually shown to my room and unpacked. I had caught a glimpse of a few of the other residents as I walked through the lounge area. I had also been seen by the doctor who had prescribed what medication I needed. One of the medications was a drug called clonidine which is really for treating high blood pressure but it reduces the withdrawal symptoms and it also has a side effect of making you dizzy when you stand up. I started my treatment that day.

I settled myself into my room and then was given some food in the dining area and met a few of the residents. I also had a timetable of where I needed to be throughout the day and most of it consisted of group therapy sessions.

I was given my medication that included amitriptyline, a strong sedative to help me sleep, and I went to bed. I wasn't allowed out of the facility even when accompanied which was a relief but I also wasn't allowed to make any phone calls or have visitors for the first ten days. Although I was relieved that I wasn't allowed out, I so much wanted to speak to Cindy and the kids even if she wasn't at all keen to speak to me. This was another reason why I needed to stay put. If I had any chance of healing some of the damage I had caused, it had to happen by me sticking this out.    Up until this point I had been living in denial of how bad things were. I didn't have a clue just how much damage I had caused and how much I had hurt this woman that had tried so hard to love me. I lived in my little fantasy world where I would think things weren't that bad but they were and I was going to find out just how bad!

My first morning started with breakfast and then a little later into my first group therapy session. I was heavily sedated and feeling the effects of the clonidine so the first few days were a blur where I couldn't talk and was finding it difficult to stay awake but was still expected to attend all the groups.

As the days passed by I became more able to participate in the groups that had about thirty of us and it was roughly fifty percent male and fifty percent female. I was trying to understand the programme they were showing us that was based on the 'twelve steps' of Alcoholics Anonymous and Narcotics Anonymous. They were treating alcoholics as well as addicts in the facility.

We would be expected to study the steps one at a time and then we would be tested in a questionnaire that was to be read out in the group and the other residents, my peers, would decide if I understood the step sufficiently to move on to the following one. It's difficult to have peers when you are under the illusion that you are special and different. I don't know how I could manage to have some sort of distorted delusion of grandeur while my arse was hanging out.

I spent most of my time in these groups during the first couple of weeks pulling people to bits in my mind. I didn't see myself as an alcoholic so that was half the group dealt with and then I went about finding reasons why most of the others were of little significance and not a bit like me. How ironic that thirty years before I was telling Dr. Williams at Porchester House that I wasn't like any of the others there for the opposite reasons and he told me that I was just like them and I would be back, and here I was just as he had predicted.

I would be challenged in so many different ways during the six weeks I was in treatment, but on one occasion I would be challenged in a way I could not have predicted and, to be honest, scared me more than anything else I had to face in there.  I had a bad tooth and had to go to the dentist. The clinic was in one of the most notorious parts of Nottingham called St Anne's. It was an area that was known for drugs, gun crime and rival gangland murders. I had frequented this area in the past but this was something so much different. I have been booked into a dentist that was right in the heart of this area and they didn't have anyone to accompany me. I was taken in a taxi but found myself having to walk some of the way on my crutches, as I made my way I could see drug deals going down around me and just felt so vulnerable. I had money in my pocket and it would have been so easy to have messed this right up but I didn't. I was sure that this was my last chance and this was my time and I was going to do whatever it took. So I put the blinkers on, did what needed to be done and managed to get back safely. When it was over I realised that this had been a big test for me and I had overcome it but I was still angry that they had put me in that situation although I didn't say anything because I didn't want to give them any excuse to throw me out. I had started off being scared of coming into this place and now I was scared of going out.

When I first came into the treatment programme I had to agree to the terms and conditions that they set out and sign a contract with the understanding that breaking this contract would result in being asked to leave. These rules and regulations made it clear that this was about doing the work provided and attending all the group therapy sessions. Obviously no drugs or alcohol use would be tolerated and violence was an automatic expulsion but one other rule was to attend the local Narcotics Anonymous (NA) or Alcoholics Anonymous (AA) meetings two or three evenings a week. I had no idea what a twelve-step programme was or an NA Meeting before I came to this place and I can't say I was over enthusiastic about it. God was mentioned too much. I think I had listened to more than enough religious teachings in my Catholic upbringing. It wouldn't take long before I started thinking it was some sort of religious cult.

As time went on, I started to grasp what they were trying to teach me but I still had that bit of defiance in me that wanted to have the last word and I thought I could do this around having to go out to the meetings. I learned that all the three NA Meetings had stairs involved and no lifts and so I said that I couldn't go to these meetings because being on crutches it wasn't safe for me and they agreed so I was feeling very smug with myself and missed the first couple, and then the other patients were coming back and saying how much they enjoyed the meeting and told me about addicts with years clean sharing their stories and making them feel really welcomed. So, now I was curious and had to go back to the powers that be and sign a disclaimer so I could attend these meetings.

Those six weeks were intense and it didn't help that I was so resistant to so many of the ideas that were put to me but I was being challenged every day, especially one counsellor in particular called Nick, who wasn't having any of my nonsense. After one particular heavy session, he came up to me and said "You might think that I am constantly having a go at you but if I see something in you that I believe could kill you I am going to go after it time and time again until you can see it too" We had a sort of love-hate relationship from then on but I knew this man had my best interests at heart.

I don't know exactly when this happened but one day they had a family day and on that day Cindy came up and also my eldest son, Steven from my first marriage. Steve and I had been spending time together before I went into the rehab and he wanted to come along. These family days were an opportunity for the family members to tell the addict how it had been for them.

This was an extremely painful experience for everyone concerned but also an extremely powerful one too. Steven said how I had never been around when he was growing up and when he was asked about what he wanted, he became very emotional and said he just wanted his dad back and then I was in tears and Cindy was consoling Steve. I don't know what Cindy said and that is not that I didn't listen but because I can't remember and I don't feel too bad about it because I just asked her about it and she can't remember either.

One of the biggest lessons I learned was when I started to grasp that first of the steps that says "We admitted we were powerless over our addiction and that our lives had become unmanageable". It was a no-brainer for me that this was true but I had to admit that I was powerless and I didn't like being powerless. I wanted to beat this even though it had kicked my butt so many times. I was then given another bit of information that hit me like a ton of bricks!   My addiction isn't concerned about what drug I use. It will react to any mind- or mood-altering chemical I put in my body and once I trigger it with one drink, one pill or one joint it will be like a snowball slowly rolling down a hill gradually picking up speed until there is no stopping it as it destroys everything in its path.

At last, I understood why time after time I would come out of prison with the best of intentions to stay clean and after a few pints of beer and a bit of this or that I would find myself sooner or later back where I started. I realised for the first time that it wasn't the last thing that I ended up using that was the problem, it was the first thing!

I was going to make more sense of all this in time but it was going to be some years down the road before that happened and for the time being I was in the right place.

I was starting to understand this stuff and it was making sense to me but I was still struggling with the God thing. Having it rammed down my throat from a young age wasn't helping but with the twelve steps it was worded in a way that I didn't slam the door on it and that was a "God of your understanding". I didn't have to know what that was right now, just be open to the idea.

I was now a willing participant in this programme and contributing more in the group sessions. When I went to the NA Meetings I was so self-conscious. At the beginning and end of each meeting there were reading cards with extracts out of the NA literature that would be read out and I would try and make sure if I didn't speak during the meeting I would at least read a card out but every time I did I would stammer and break out in a cold sweat that soaked me. I needed to push myself because otherwise I might never have said a word and I was going to have to keep these up after the treatment. It was reassuring to hear people just like me talking about all the things I had felt and done and seeing some of those same people years away from their last drug and what's more they seemed happy! There was real hope for me in those rooms and I could feel it.

When I first came into this treatment centre I had no idea what to expect but I was out of options. Deep down, I knew I had nowhere else to go. I was broken and beaten but- guess what?- as soon as I was feeling a bit better I started getting cocky and questioning everything and then telling them why they couldn't make me go to meetings. A lot of the residents were a lot younger than me and hadn't done the things I had done so I would tell my stories and impress them with my exploits and have my ego stroked for a while. It wasn't helpful and it would be all about good times and conveniently leaving the bad bits out and exaggerating the good times for effect. I loved the attention but when I look at it now it is embarrassing and thankfully I started to realise what I was doing and moved away from this bullshit, and I started to become teachable, I wanted to soak up as much of this education as possible.

This is where my search for the truth began. This was the beginning of a new paradigm for me that would eventually uncover who I truly was but it was early days and these were my first baby steps.

I was getting visits from Cindy and the kids during this time on a Saturday afternoon and I had told the kids that I was in a hospital because of the injury to my leg but Simone who was eleven soon noticed that no one else seemed injured and asked me why? I made some excuses but I knew I would need to be honest with them on the next visit. So when they next came I told them I needed to tell them something and explained that I was in there because I had a drug problem and I wanted to stop. Simone piped up straight away that she knew I was using drugs but Theresa was quiet and Jack, too. He was only eight and perhaps he didn't fully understand but I was glad that it was out in the open and I didn't need to lie to them anymore.

The programme, as I have previously said, was based on the twelve steps of AA or as in my case NA but there wasn't enough time to take us through all twelve of the steps so we were taken through the first four steps.

Step one is… "We admitted we were powerless over our addiction and that our lives had become unmanageable"

Step two is…. "Came to believe a power greater than ourselves could restore us to sanity"

Step three is… "Made a decision to turn our will and our lives over to the care of God as we understood Him"

I had completed these three and it was explained simply like this… Don't pick up that first drug you are powerless over it, and believe in something else working in your life. That wasn't too hard for me because I had seen things happen that I had no part in and yet this was why I found myself in there. As for God, I was told that all I needed to know about God was "It isn't you, Son!" I had been running the show in the past and the results spoke for themselves as I was about to be shown in the next step.

Step four is… "Made a searching and fearless moral inventory of ourselves"

I didn't find out until later that what I was being asked to do in there was nothing like a real step four. What it ended up being was a long list of all the things that had been done to me and all the things I had done to other people. Some of these things I had not spoken to another human being about in all of my forty-seven years and after it was done I was expected to read it out in front of the counsellor and about forty residents that were young enough to be my children.

I was convinced that this had to be done and if I didn't do it or left anything out I would most probably relapse and go back to my drug using, so I never thought I had a choice. After all, these were professionals and knew what they were doing… or so I thought.

It came to the fateful morning and as I went into the group therapy room feeling like a condemned man. The chairs were set out in the usual way a circle and I would be sitting next to the counselor. That gave me a degree of comfort. We went through the usual morning readings to ground us and then it was over to me to read my confession! I mean, 'step four'. The room began to fill up and I became more nervous and all I could think was to just get it done and get out of there.

I began reading and I guess it lasted about forty minutes. I was feeling extremely emotional and raw and then the counsellor, I think it was Nick, asked the group if they had any feedback for me. Most of it was comforting and supporting and then a young lad piped up and said "Wow! It just sounded like a James Cagney film!" I had just poured my heart out with my deepest darkest secrets and this is what he came up with. To this day, I don't know how I stayed in my seat but thank goodness I did because I was full of rage and would have done him some serious damage if I had reacted. I was so distraught after it was over and done with. An elderly counsellor called Patrick came up to me and hugged me and said something that stayed with me and that was this: "One day Trevor all this will just be a story". He said it in such a way that I had no doubts that he knew this was possible and I was desperate for that to be true for me, and today it is. I was going to uncover something that would be a major turning point in my recovery and the quality of my life in so many ways but how that came about comes later in the book.

When I had time to process what had happened that day I thought it was not only brutally cruel but dangerous. I didn't know about having abreactions and re-traumatising someone when working through traumas, but that evening after I had presented that step work I experienced some strange goings on that worried me. I was in the lounge area and a few people were sitting around a large table when everything seemed to become somewhat surreal. My vision became a bit blurred when people spoke it sounded as if it was coming from another room and sounded far away. I felt a sense of disconnection and I had no idea why it was happening. I didn't say anything to anyone. I didn't want to be on my own in case it got any worse; I was fearing the worst and thought it might be some sort of permanent damage. I was relieved when it began to subside and I felt safe enough to go to bed.

I think I got away lightly because I can remember a young girl who had been put through the same thing as me and who had experienced lots of childhood sexual abuse and she had been confined to her bed with twenty-four hour supervision and it took her four days to come out of her abreaction. She told me later that she had gone into herself to escape the memories and feelings and I now know that this is referred to as disassociation and remembered doing it myself at times when I was being attacked by my dad. It was my safe place and felt very much what I had experienced a couple of days before.

So, now it was time for me to leave the safety of the unit and go back home and although I wanted to go home, I was full of fear. This was the real test for me and my track record wasn't good. Whenever I have been left to my own devices sooner or later I have messed up and that very nearly happened this time!

# 17
## MY LAST RELAPSE

I thought in the beginning that I only had a drug problem. In fact, I only believed that I had a problem with a couple of drugs really: crack cocaine and heroin. I thought all I needed to do was get through the detox in the clinic and my life would return to normal. Well, I was in for a rude awakening. I had started to realise through the NA Meetings that it was a hell of a lot more than that but I had no concept of how big a job I had in front of me.

When I first arrived home there was a sort of honeymoon period and I don't mean between Cindy and I. It was about being clean for the first time in years and having hope for the future but that honeymoon period was short lived. I was riddled with guilt. I now had my feelings back and no anesthetic! There were three NA Meetings in Nottingham at the time and I was making sure I went to them all. I had been told I needed to get myself a sponsor; this was someone who would help me work through the steps and who I could phone at any time if I was struggling.

I was doing all the things that were suggested and I had a list of phone numbers of other members that became part of my support team. I was putting all these things in place but it was starting to dawn on me how much damage I had done. I looked around the house and saw how I had neglected it. I had half-finished jobs, a car I had been meaning to repair in the back garden, and my dogs that I had neglected and were in bad shape. All this was nothing compared to what I had done to my family. I had no relationship with Cindy as such, I had put her through hell and I didn't know if I could ever repair that damage. To be honest, I am not sure if I wanted to at that time. I just wanted to run but I wanted it to be someone else's fault; I needed an excuse.

I had this attitude of "Can't she see how hard I am trying?" as if I had some sort of entitlement to be forgiven. What is the point of putting all this effort into staying clean if I am getting no recognition for it? This is how self-centered I was. It was all about me.

One night I did the unthinkable, on the pretense of going to a meeting I decided "I've had enough of all this" and I went to my dealer in Edwinstowe. I scored, smoked some crack and then the moment I had done it I was filled with even more guilt. We had gone to another house to use it and when we got back to the dealer's place he told me the brown (heroin) had arrived and invited me in. As soon as the effects of crack wear off, you are left with a feeling of having every last nerve on edge and an unbelievable craving to get more and at this point the only thing that can take the edge off it is more crack (that was no longer available) or heroin. So, I find myself standing on this dealer's doorstep on the verge of making a decision that could sabotage everything. It is a cold, dark winter night; his house looks warm and has an inviting glow about it. I can see the log fire burning as I glance through the front window. I am walking up the drive to the front door, with all these feelings coursing through me and at that point no idea which way this was going to go. Then, from somewhere inside me I hear a small voice that is telling me: "If you cross that threshold it is game over and there are no more second chances". In that moment I made a decision, I needed to stand on my own two feet and deal with whatever recovery threw at me. I needed to man up. I needed to take responsibility for my own recovery. It wasn't up to anyone else and I can't keep blaming other people or circumstances for my woes. So, I reached the door and was told the brown was there and I was invited in but for the first time in my life, I said 'no'. I turned around, walked away, got into my car and drove away. That is well over twenty years ago now and I have never used drugs or alcohol since.

I knew that there had been a major shift in me that night; someone was still watching over me but that wasn't going to help me explain to Cindy why my sponsor had rung up to ask her why I hadn't shown up at the meeting. So I did what I always do when I get caught out, I lied through my teeth with some excuse saying I just needed some time on my own. I don't think trying to explain to her I had some sort of epiphany after smoking crack would have gone down too well. I knew I had to get honest with her at some point and so I took the coward's way out and saw my counselor, Julie at the rehab. She arranged a meeting for us to come in together and that's where I told Cindy, and here I was again after all my promises. I had let her down again and I was so ashamed of myself as I watched her sobbing in despair but deep down inside I knew something had changed in me.

It was time for me to start and I threw myself into working with my sponsor trying to do the right thing and not expecting anything in return. I was going to have to earn trust. I was still this selfish, self-centred son of a bitch that was still doing things that were so cruel. Cindy overheard me talking to a female NA member about how we were struggling around our relationship and when she confronted me about it and I could see how betrayed she felt, I was just so dismissive and told her it was none of her business, that I needed to talk about it and that the NA people understood how I was feeling.

I was starting to see parts of my personality that were plain ugly and this one particular trait I realised was one I had used from a young age was that if I am feeling emotional pain I will purposely try to hurt the person who I think caused it more than they hurt me. It was a conscious decision to hurt Cindy or make her jealous because I was hurting. I was feeling rejected and I am sad to say I did it quite a few times in different ways but with no regard for the fact that Cindy had every right to feel and act the way she did towards me. Her feelings are my consequences for how I had been treating her for years.

Over time, I began to identify so many more of these traits that I used in certain situations that may have been classed as a survival skill in some of the environments that I had experienced, but they had no place in my life now and made it impossible to make any real progress in my relationships or life in general. I was still living in the past.

As time went on, I was feeling more and more like a fish out of water. I had stopped taking drugs but I was still angry and losing my temper at the slightest thing. I was still out of the house a lot of the time by either being at work or going to my meetings. Besides the fact that I wasn't using drugs, nothing had changed. In fact, it had become worse. I had no communication skills; if Cindy tried to talk to me about how she was feeling, I went straight to the defensive and wouldn't listen. I think we both came close to giving up on each other. I can remember an occasion after one of our many arguments when I announced that I thought it would be a good idea if I moved into a bedsit, somewhere, where I could just concentrate on my recovery. I was sure this would have the desired result and she would see the error of her ways and beg me not to go but alas it never went that way and she blurted out "GOOD! I will help you pack!" followed by a few expletives! At which time I realised my plan was somewhat flawed and I immediately went into some nifty back-peddling to save the day.

I never realised it at the time but I had the meetings, my support network, we even had conventions in places like Bournemouth where hundreds of recovering addicts would meet and listen to three days of people with twenty and thirty years of recovery sharing on stage how they did it. It was an amazing atmosphere and I would come away feeling empowered. I went to at least one or two every year. I had all this support and Cindy had nothing. She had nowhere to go and I was as usual only concerned about myself. It wasn't until one day she told me how I ended up in rehab that I had any real idea of what Cindy was going through at that time. Don't get me wrong, I knew it was bad but I never had the courage to ask her how bad. She told me that during that last year of my using she would be sitting at home on her own after the kids were put to bed and she would be waiting for a knock on the door and the police saying I was dead from either an overdose or a car accident. She had watched me deteriorate during that time and was convinced that this was going to be the inevitable outcome.

Although Cindy had her mum and a sister living in Newark, she was too ashamed to talk to them about me. Her mum at that time was in her seventies. One day, out of desperation, she went to see my brother instead and told him how bad things had become. That's when

Alan contacted me. I never knew until then that Cindy was the one who had started the ball rolling that would get me into that rehab. Hearing her say how she was sat every night with that fear of that knock at the door, it shocked me. I had always believed that the only person I was harming was myself and that I was the only one that suffered the consequences of what I was doing. This lie was a hard pill to swallow even though the evidence now was clear for me to see. I wanted to believe it. I wanted absolution! I am now left with more questions than answers. Why am I incapable of understanding how my actions impacted on other people especially those I love? I had not only done a good job of overcoming my negative emotions with drugs; now I was drug free all I seemed to be able to feel are anger and blame. Where was the good stuff like empathy and compassion and love? I was beginning to think I had done myself some permanent brain damage because this wasn't normal.

I instinctively knew that my problems stemmed from my past and I wanted to do another 'step four' to make a 'searching and fearless moral inventory' but this time in the right way. This time it would be with one person, my sponsor. I was hoping this would be the answer to so many of my questions. I didn't relish the thought of going through my life story again but I felt I needed to and I had completed the previous three steps and this was the next in line. I was about to get started on it when I had a call to start a job in Avonmouth, near Bristol. I thought this was perfect as I knew I would be a nightmare to live with while I worked through these difficult memories and I didn't want to cause any more hurt to Cindy. This was going to be hard and I knew I would be lashing out in various ways but I also thought that these contractors that I didn't know were fair game and so they could deal with me. It was the best I could come up with at the time!

I arrived on the site and was told I would be on the night shift. They had accommodation arranged in a house with multiple bedrooms and a shared bathroom and kitchen. I had the house to myself during the day and soon had a routine going. I would leave work at six in the morning straight to the transport café for breakfast, eight hours sleep, get up and do some step work and then get something to eat before going to work. I did four nights and then travelled home Friday morning.

It was going ok but as I came to painful parts in my step work I found myself having more arguments at work to the point that I nearly came to blows with one guy. I just carried on doing my step four and tried to keep my mouth shut at work. On one of my trips back home I was feeling really emotional and I always stopped halfway home for a coffee and a snack. As I sat in a corner of the café just fighting back tears as the memories and feelings that I had been working through that week came flooding back, I happened to see a few people on a table not far from me and one of the people was in a wheelchair and looked as if he had motor neuron disease. As I watched him struggling to communicate with the others, I just had this overwhelming feeling of "How dare I sit here feeling sorry for myself?" I was so humbled by this man's courage and it made my own struggles pale into insignificance by comparison. I wanted to let him know how much he had helped me and I went over to their table on my way out and I must have mentioned Steven Hawking and one of the ladies with him said the two of them were friends. I have often thought of him and more so when I have my bouts of self-pity. He was put in front of me for a purpose that day and I was so grateful.

I went back to that job for a few weeks. I had managed to find an NA meeting that was open at lunchtime and was a chance to connect with new NA members. I eventually finished that step four and not long after that

I gave in my notice; the job had served its purpose.

I was hopeful that writing this step and then working through it with my sponsor in step five was going to be some sort of magic bullet and all the memories and feelings about my childhood would be taken away, but they weren't and I came to realise it was never supposed to be that way.

These steps helped me get a better understanding of the areas of my life that were causing me problems, my strengths and weaknesses and taking ownership of the part I played in certain situations. It was an education. I was also doing service in the Fellowship and became the chair of the Public Information Committee, which involved talking to professionals about what NA was and what it did. Then I did some work for the Hospitals and Institutions Committee, started a meeting up in a prison and chaired one in Nottingham prison.

I was always thinking of all the people I knew who had never heard of NA. I wanted to find one in particular and that was Frizzel. I don't know why because he had dropped me in it on more than one occasion but we had been through a lot together. I hadn't seen him for a few years now and at one point I went to where I had heard he last worked. It was a garden centre in Lincoln, but I never found him. I had almost given up hope when one day at a meeting at the Health Shop in Nottingham he walked in. He had been in a detox facility that NA had an arrangement with, for anyone who wanted to attend an NA meeting. We would have someone pick them up, take them to the meeting and drop them back there after the meeting was over. Well, when I saw him I rushed over and gave him the biggest bear hug that he resisted until he realised who I was. We both ended up in tears.

Mick had some good years in NA. I sponsored him for a while and he was doing really well. He became involved in the service committees. I remember one day we were out with a few other members having a picnic and fishing at a local lake on a beautiful summer's day and he said to me "Who would have thought after all the places we have been and the things we have done that we would be laid here together talking about a Higher Power?"

Mick would get a few years under his belt and then relapse and it usually was around a relationship. He would then come back and start again and do the same thing. He had moved away from Nottingham now and was part of NA in other areas. After a while he came back to live in a homeless hostel and was using again. Shortly afterwards, he was rushed to hospital after injecting in his groin and lost his leg below the knee. I visited him and he wanted to give recovery another go so when he got out we started working together. Mick had a lot of trauma from his early days in detention centres and borstal. Deep down, he knew that this was his nemesis. He was doing well but he had some personal issues that he couldn't come to terms with. One day he relapsed, and this was his last one because a few months later he passed away.

When Mick first came into that meeting in Nottingham, I had taken up a new sponsor. His name was Pete and he lived in Louth, which was forty-five miles from me. Quite a trek! My first visit was to formally ask him if he would be my sponsor. I had first seen him doing a Public Information workshop in Nottingham and was impressed with his knowledge of NA and its history but there was something else about him that attracted me, too. It might have been his calm, peaceful presence. A friend of mine came over to me after the workshop and said to me "He would be a good sponsor for you" so that clinched it and I took the plunge. I asked him and that's when he invited me to his house to discuss it.

I pulled up outside his house and he invited me into the front room and made me a cup of tea. Pointing to a dresser with a row of about twenty books on, the first thing Pete said to me was "those are my journals". So, from that first statement he was not telling me what to do but he was sowing seeds. While we were talking, Pete told me he was a single parent and had a young daughter, Willow. He was from a Romany background. Newark has a large Romany and Traveller community so I had been around them all my life and quite a few of my friends were Travellers. We would have fun talking in Romany or the bits I had picked up over the years. While I was there I couldn't help but notice that he didn't have any carpets down and I asked him about it and he simply said "I haven't decided if I am stopping yet" He had been used to living in a traditional 'bow top' caravan and this was all new to him.

Pete became a major influence in my life and a good friend to this day. He taught me so much about humility, acceptance, forgiveness and being of service to others and more besides; all the areas that I was lacking in at that time. He was passionate about Public Information and he would do presentations to prisons, hospitals or anywhere where it was needed. I can remember he once took us to a village church meeting and he found it amusing because Mick was there singing away to the hymns, just like he would at the prison services and I was looking real uncomfortable because of my Catholic upbringing and my aversion to religions.

Pete taught me a lot and I was asked to do a PI Presentation for something called at that time "The Crime and Disorder Partnership" at a place called Kelham Hall that was just outside Newark. This is a beautiful hall and gardens that was first built in the mid 1600s. The presentation was to take place in the Great Chapel, a large domed masterpiece spanning sixty-two feet across and sixty-eight feet high.

As we walked into this formidable but beautiful setting with its columns and enormous oak tables with all these dignitaries sat around them, I suddenly realised that I had been in the Great Chapel before. I had been there thirty years ago when I was brought to visit the monks when I had been in the Porchester House rehab. I was now sitting in front of quite a big panel of people from different organisations such as the probation service, three divisions of the police force and someone from the Home Office, so no pressure…

We did our presentation and it was well received and afterwards while we were chatting to different people a man came over to me and said "You don't remember me, do you?" and I said "No, sorry, I don't" and he told me that he was a retired police officer who now chaired this partnership. When he received our request to do a presentation and he saw my name on it he agreed for us to come because he couldn't believe I was clean and wanted to see for himself.

Things were getting better at home but we still had a long way to go. My anger and sometimes uncontrollable rage would raise its ugly head every now and again, as in the case of street brawl with a neighbour. I was at the time about three years clean and under the illusion that these days were a thing of the past. On this occasion, it was around playing music loudly. Well, it was more to do with that music that has a heavy base beat that just seems to be constant and inescapable. It had been going on for a while and I had felt myself getting angry and had gone into town to escape it and not lose my temper. When I returned all was quiet, thankfully, but I wouldn't have to wait long before it started again and so I went across to his house and asked him to turn it down and he did but a few minutes later it was up again and at that point my jacket was off and I was marching across the road.

The neighbour had a couple of mates with him and his two sons. Steve, my eldest son was there with Cindy and our kids had come out of the house. I called this neighbour out and the fight started. It went on for a while and ended when I was on top of him and one of his sons ran up, kicked me in the face and ran off. I got up and when I looked around Jack, our youngest who was about ten then, was crying. I asked him "Why are you crying?" and he said to me "This doesn't mean you are going back to prison again does it, Dad?" I told him, " 'Course not, Son", but I was left in shock because maybe for the first time in my life I was seeing how my behaviour was hurting the ones I loved. The other thing was that I thought because he was so young he wouldn't have been affected so much with me being locked up. I was wrong.

My neighbour and I ended up at the hospital but when I got back I sat down with Jack and talked to him. During that chat, I made a promise to him, which was that from that day, no matter what, I will never lift my hand to another human being and no excuses. I made that promise to him more than twenty years ago and as I write this I am proud to say I have kept that promise to him. I won't say it has been easy. I have been tested on more than one occasion.

It was about this time that I was going to get another rude awakening about my lack of empathy and thoughtlessness. I didn't know at the time but Cindy had made contact with my counselor, Julie from the clinic about the difficulties we were having in our relationship. One of the suggestions was that we see another counsellor called Audrey and so we both went along. I don't know how many times we saw her but one meeting in particular sticks in my mind. She asked me, "If you were out shopping with Cindy and someone knocked Cindy to the ground and stole her purse, what would you do?" Without hesitation I said, "Chase the robber and get her purse back" and Audrey said "What about Cindy?" In a split second, I realised how selfish I was and how not for one moment did I think of Cindy and if she was hurt. It was more about "How dare he?" I wanted to catch him, punish him and get the purse back. I wanted to return the hero carrying the spoils but ended up learning a valuable lesson. I don't know if it makes sense to anyone else but it was a major learning curve for me and I won't ever forget it.

We were about to go on our first holiday abroad. I was working and earning well so we booked a holiday on a Greek Island, Skiathos. It was a lovely holiday. Jack and Simone were about eleven and fourteen respectively. We were dropped off at our little villa by a bus, dropped our bags off and headed straight to the beach that was just across the road from us. It was sunny, the sands were white, the sea was blue and as we paddled little fish swam around our feet. It was towards the end of the season and we had the beach to ourselves.

We really had a good time and it was a time that we healed some of our wounds. We hired a couple of mopeds to get about on, spent lots of time on the beach and would go into the small town in the evening and sample the local cuisine. When we got back to our villa at night we would lay out and look at the stars. We had a great time and it did us all the world of good. Theresa, our eldest, didn't come; she was in her twenties by that time and in a relationship so had left the nest.

Life was improving and we were about to have some good news that was going to make a huge difference to our lives.

# 18
## THE WAR IS OVER

The holiday we took together showed me how life could be. We laid on the beach, soaked up the sun, swam in the sea and had fish swimming around our feet, and we ate good food together. I was reminded of hearing a guy talking about his life as an addict and as he reached the end of it he said to us all, "The war is over, you lost, welcome home." Laid on that beach with my family around me gave me a sense of that but I felt that once I returned home the war would still be there and the battles would continue. I felt as if I had been in conflict my whole life and even though I was clean now I was still having problems with my neighbours, people at work, the union conflicts that cropped up now and again, going on anti-racism marches, conflicts with my wife and children. Even in NA, I was having fallouts. At one of the business meetings someone had said something I found offensive and before I knew it I had him by the throat on the floor. I was tired of it but I hadn't found the answer yet.

My sponsor said to me one day, "If you are so tired of fighting and being in conflict why do you keep getting back in the ring?" I was beginning to understand what he meant but I wasn't there yet. Self-righteousness and anger were not a good combination and I had more than my fair share of both at that time.

It didn't help that I was living in the same house that I had used drugs in for all those years and it held all the memories of what I had done in that house. I was surrounded by other addicts that all knew me and expected me to fail. We lived on a council estate at that time and when I first started using hard drugs like heroin, I could count on one hand how many others were doing the same thing. As I was the main supplier at that time, I was able to keep a tight rein on them and didn't let them sell anything outside of our small group. It was about self-preservation. The last thing I wanted was any more attention from the police. Now this was a thing of the past and the whole estate was rife with drugs of one description or another and was well and truly out of control. It seemed as if every street corner had a dealer but it was a different breed and a lot of them had no scruples about how they got their money. Robberies, burglaries on people's homes, even robbing each other. Some were known as 'knockers' and would travel around the country looking for people who had antiques and talking them into selling them at a fraction of what they were worth and then selling them on to antique dealers.

The estate was getting more dangerous and gangs were roaming around at night and my son, Jack told me one day that he had been chased by some lads with knives. I had to get me and my family out of there. One day when Cindy was stripping some wallpaper in one of the bedrooms we noticed a big crack in the wall and called the council out to have a look at it. They reported back to us that the breezeblocks had a defect and the walls were crumbling. It wasn't just one wall so we would have to move out while they did the repairs and made it safe. This seemed like a blessing in disguise and they started sending details of properties for us to look at. We had viewed two and had turned them down because one was in the same neighbourhood and the other was too small and no parking, but then something spooky was about to happen. Cindy was travelling back from a car boot sale with our eldest daughter Theresa and as she was passing Kelham Hall she pointed out a row of six houses opposite a farm and said to

Theresa, "Those sort of houses are so hard to come by and you never see them vacant." This was on a Sunday, and the very next day she got a phone call from the council saying one of those six houses was about to be vacated and would we be interested in it? We were dumbfounded, it was unbelievable and we were so excited; it was beyond our wildest dreams. It came to light that one of the current elderly residents had had an accident that made it impossible for him to navigate the stairs and he had to move into a bungalow in town. We just could not believe our luck. We now had a house in the country with a garden front and back and the back one looked out over fields and a river close by.

Our excitement was not shared by our stroppy teenage son who wasn't keen to move into 'the middle of nowhere' as he put it, and away from all his friends. He had no transport and so I had to compromise and became a taxi for him. I didn't mind and this was not just good for Cindy and I but it was going to be good for Jack, too. He just couldn't see it yet. At that time Theresa, our eldest was in her twenties and was in a relationship and living with her then-boyfriend. Simone was nineteen and had moved in with her boyfriend. Jack was sixteen.

This was our chance to make a fresh start; a safe place for me and my family. I had a good job and we could start making plans. I don't think we had been moved in long when Jack started smoking weed. It was that skunk weed and so every time he came in the house his clothes would wreak of it. We had more than enough arguments about this, he was young and was full of anger. He had no respect for me at that time and I could understand why, but I couldn't have him bringing drugs into the house and eventually he agreed not to, so I just had to live with that for a while. The truth was I was scared. I was so frightened he was going to end up going down a road just like mine and I felt responsible. How could I tell him he can't smoke weed after what I had been doing for the past thirty years? My words carried no weight with him and the alternative was to tell him to leave and I couldn't do that either. I just needed to be there for him, and I needed to practice unconditional love and it wasn't easy but we also needed to set boundaries with him and not bringing drugs into the house was the first. This was all new territory for me. I had never had boundaries myself and now I was setting them for my son!

Not long after this, Jack had a motorcycle accident and broke his femur. He was lucky that he was with friends that night because when he lost control he had ended up in a flooded dyke and his friends jumped down and supported his head until the ambulance arrived and then when they did arrive wouldn't climb down to him because of health and safety concerns, even though he was shouting out in agony. He then had to wait for the fire brigade to rescue him before he could be taken to hospital and later have a rod fitted into the broken femur.

On one occasion while he was in hospital and hooked up to morphine he had his own button where he could press it at will if he was in pain. When we were visiting him one evening he asked me to press the button for him and I remember how uncomfortable I felt doing that, administering morphine to my son felt so wrong in spite of the circumstances. Anyway, on this occasion after he came out of hospital we realised that he was going to be bed ridden for some time, so we decided to move his bed down into the front room for him and his friends would come and visit him most days. I was so grateful for those good friends of his that stayed with him that night of the accident. By the time I found out and managed to get there he was already in the back of the ambulance.

As I mentioned before, Jack was no stranger to A&E in Newark and was on first-name terms with some of the nurses. It was a time when BMX bikes were all the rage and he would be a regular on the tracks but accidents were all part of it. He had a more serious accident when he was only about three years old involving a milk float. The milkman used to let the kids ride in the float with him for a short way to the end of the cul-de-sac when we were still living in the old house on the estate and Jack fell out and was injured. I can remember each time I have been told that Jack has had an accident, how frightened I was and not knowing how bad it was but this time when he was just a toddler and was the worst, I will never forget that journey as long as I live. I was working at a power station on the outskirts of Nottingham and he had been taken to the Queen's Medical Centre, which is also in Nottingham, but that ten miles to the hospital seemed like a hundred miles as I drove at breakneck speeds with my heart in my mouth. I had been told he had been run over by a milk float and I knew that ours at the time were the milk floats that are battery powered and weigh at least a ton and I was fearing the worst and terrified of what I was going to discover at the other end.

When I arrived at the hospital and found them, Cindy told me how just before he was taken to be X-rayed he said to her "Don't cry, Mummy. I will be alright." It still brings a lump to my throat and a tear to my eye when I think about it. We were at the hospital for some time and I was feeling powerless and useless and at that time I was still using so I had all the guilt around that. After what seemed like an eternity, the doctor came to us to explain that Jack had a greenstick fracture to his pelvis but that they wouldn't have to operate because it would heal on its own. What a relief, I could have kissed the doctor that day, even though he was a man!

After Jack's motorbike accident he was in bed for quite a few weeks and a terrible patient. Even when he was in the hospital he was a pain in the butt and often on my way in to visit him I would be called into the office and asked to have a word with Jack about his attitude and how he spoke to the nurses. I did as they asked but I don't think I was very successful and in all honesty I think they were pleased to see him go.

During this time I was still going to NA meetings and working with Pete, my sponsor. I was really enjoying the Public Information work and it was about this time that I saw a job advertised in a prison with RAPT. This was a charity and RAPT stood for the 'Rehabilitation of Addicted Prisoners Trust' and mainly took prisoners through the twelve steps of NA. They were advertising for a counsellor and I rang up to ask about it and was encouraged to come along and experience being in front of a panel even if I didn't have the qualifications for the job, so this is what I did.

I answered all their questions on the day and set off home. On my way home, I had a phone call and it was one of those on the panel members who informed me that they were so impressed with my interview that they wanted to create a post for me as a trainee RAPT Counsellor and would I be interested? I was so excited at the prospect and immediately said, "Yes!"

My excitement was short lived when I was told the governor of the prison had turned my application for clearance down on the grounds of my previous record although at the time my last conviction was twenty years ago and I was also at that time chairing an NA Meeting in Nottingham Prison. I was bitterly disappointed and it seemed so unfair but I was told that security clearance was up to the individual governors or security officers.

I was trying to get rid of the chips on my shoulder but I would add this one for a little while. So, it was back to the power stations. I was ready for a change and I was about to do something that would burn my bridges with power station work for a few years. Around

2000, I started with a firm called Mitsui Babcocks at Cottam Power Station and there was a dispute about pay. To take it any further we needed to nominate a shop steward, and nobody wanted to take it on because in those days it could easily be the end of your career. Although being 'blacked' was illegal, it didn't stop it happening and it was a hard thing to prove but I was not too concerned because I was ready for something new. I was tired of just being a number. I wanted something new; my life was changing and I was becoming more enthusiastic about my future.

I put my hand up, volunteered and was quickly voted in, as was my friend John Moran as the deputy steward. We were addressing about two hundred men in the car park and the vote was to strike. This strike went on for a few weeks while we negotiated with the management with the help of our union official. We had timed this action well and had been sure that the station was inoperable when we made our demands and in the end they caved in and gave us everything we asked for. It was a great victory for us. If I remember correctly, all our shift money was increased but the night shifts money had nearly doubled. I don't know how true it was but I heard that Mitsui Babcocks lost £250,000 on that contract, so my bridges were good and truly burned. John went on to work with other contractors but I didn't try. I was done with them for good, or so I thought but that would change some years later when I would return for a while.

Things were improving and I had been clean for a few years now and was starting to do things that were never possible before, like going for family holidays and not worrying about a methadone script and whatever else I would need to take with me. I was free at last and enjoying every minute.

My dogs had long gone by now and I had always wanted to own a bird of prey, a hawk and that happened for me. I bought a Harris Hawk from a dealer and falconer in Hull. She was twenty weeks old when I purchased her and she had been parent-reared, this meant she had never seen a human until the day I went to collect her. The falconer, Clive, helped me put her anklets and jesses on and we were ready to go. I had built her pen (mews) and went through the training that took about six weeks and then came the fateful day when I would fly her free and hope she came back. I had visions of my £350 disappearing over the horizon but it all went well and I had some wonderful times with her. I named her Leia after the princess in 'Star Wars'. I also had a few ferrets, too and they worked together. Leia was smart enough to know not to harm them when they were working and they became a team. I had always loved hunting and we would catch a couple of rabbits or pheasants, just enough for a meal for both of us and then we would head home.

Home life was getting better but there was still a lot of healing work left to do. I was becoming more aware of how inept I was of having a healthy relationship and we had been advised by someone to organise a date night and there were some rules on these date nights that had to be adhered to. They would be a weekly affair and during the evening one of us would get a chance to say whatever was on their minds that was a problem for them or causing them to become stressed or angry. It could be anything the other person might have done or said that week or not done or said that week but the main thing was that they could freely speak without interruptions or tuts or looking at the ceiling, just listening. I don't know if Cindy found it as difficult as I did but we persevered and we both agreed that this was one of the best things we could have done to start the healing of our relationship. We both learned to really listen to each other and we were making progress. The main ingredient of all this was that we both wanted this to work and we were both by this time committed to finding a way through it. I was learning how to court my wife for the first time after twelve years of marriage; this really was a new start and I thought intimacy was sex! I found that having an intimate relationship with anyone was about honesty, being vulnerable, something I had avoided at all costs, admitting when I was scared or didn't know something. As we built our relationship, learned to trust again and heal those wounds from the past it had a positive effect on the rest of the family.

There were still parts of me that I didn't like, such as my anger. Sometimes it would grow into rage and I had a real hard time trying to control it. One incident from the past that I remember clearly was when Jack was sat halfway up the stairs at the old house and at that time he was only about ten years old. I had lost my temper with him over something and he was crying and asked him why are you crying and he said "You are going to hit me" and this just made me more angry. I remember saying "Why would you say such a thing, I have never hit you", and he said "Yes but I think you are". I suddenly realised in that moment how scary I must look to a child when I lose my temper; for Christ sake I can scare grown men! It didn't matter that I didn't hit my kids the way I spoke to them and scared them was just as damaging. I was desperate not to be like this and I didn't have a clue how I was going to stop it happening again, I needed help and I was searching for it and accumulating an admirable collection of self-help books in the process.

I was about to start working for a new employer, British Waterways. This was a complete change for me and the new start I was looking for. I was working in a small dry dock in the town centre next to the town locks and the castle. It was in complete contrast to what I had been used to in the past. Power station work was extremely hot and dusty, even though the boiler we were working on would be off, we might well be in between two that were full on and together with the fact that these repairs always happened in the summer months, you can imagine how bad the conditions could be. Now here I was, in this dry dock and workshops with the river running down both sides of us, and clean work.

I loved my time there. It wasn't anywhere near the wages I was used to but it was enough for us to live quite comfortably on. The work was interesting. We were building small workboats that are used to clear silt from the riverbed. There had been a time when we got a contract to build some big office barges that would be sold and transported to London's Paddington Basin to use as floating office space. These were big projects and there were only two

platers- myself and my friend Tony Joynes.
Part of our job was also building and welding
the arms that went on manually opening lock
gates, so we had a variety of work and
sometimes we would go out to small locks in
thirty-mile radius of us to carry out repairs.
There was something about working near
rivers with all the nature that surrounded us; I
was really enjoying it out there. The rest of the
crew consisted of about eight others that were
involved in the mechanical side of things, such
as fitting the boats out and they were really
nice people to work with. We didn't have
managers on the site; they were based in
Wakefield and would come down once a week
and check things out and that was the only
time we would see them. I felt valued and
respected while I was working there. This was
not how I felt when working as a contractor
on the power stations; we were just there to
do a job and when it was over you were made
redundant and if you had time off for any
reason you would be sacked, and if you
stepped out of line you were laid off for some
made-up reason. There was a lot of money to
be earned on those jobs but it was a dog-eat-
dog environment and it wasn't unusual to be
made redundant two or three times in a year. I
had been doing that too long. This new job
was a breath of fresh air for me.

Jack was recovering nicely from his motorbike injury and was now in a wheelchair. After the accident involving the milk float all those years ago, Jack had been awarded compensation that had been put into a trust until his eighteenth birthday and that day had arrived. We would take him out on shopping trips to buy new clothes and trainers in his wheelchair. Once he was mobile, he passed his test and bought a car so that he could get about; up until then he had relied on scooters and the ill-fated motorbike that he didn't seem too keen to return to and I was relieved to know that.

Cindy was also going to find a new job and take her career in a totally different direction. She had been working for the MOD for thirteen years in administration, and one day we had an invite to come and look around a new residential rehab that was about to be opened and was going to be run by some people from the Nottingham rehab that I had been through. So we went along and I have to admit that I was expecting that I might be offered a job but what actually happened was something else. We were shown around and it really was in a beautiful setting in a small village, and consisted of a fourteen-bedroomed Victorian manor house set in a couple of acres of wonderful gardens. As we were being shown around, it became apparent that what they were most in need of was a chef and although Cindy wasn't a qualified chef she was an excellent cook and was soon offered the job. She accepted it, resigned from the MOD and started her new career at what was now to be called Lynwode Manor and she soon worked her way through the ranks and eventually came to manage it.

At this time I had been at my Waterways job for five years but it was about to come to an end. One day, we were told it was going to be shut down. It was a shock and we never expected it. I was used to jobs coming to an end but disappointed at the same time. Most of the other men (not counting Tony) had been there since they left school and even though they were mostly in their late fifties or early sixties they were clearly affected and angry that they were after all these years to be made redundant. They needed a shop steward as theirs had recently retired and as I was the only one with any experience and asked to take his place. I was duly nominated and elected. This was a lot different to my last experience with Matsui Babcocks. This was only a matter of trying to get the best redundancy package they could and the managers were really helping that happen. We had been doing overtime up until then and this was going to enhance the calculation of their pension, so the managers allowed it to continue right up until the last day. When they saw their figures before finally leaving they were all very happy.

I received a nice package too and Cindy and I decided to have a special holiday together. Cindy is Malaysian and was born in a place called Malacca and she had left there when she was only eighteen months old and never been back. We made plans to visit the house where she was born. It was going to be an epic trip.

We had already had our wedding blessed two years earlier at St Wilfred's, a small medieval church in the grounds of Kelham Hall for our 20th wedding anniversary. We were surrounded by all our friends and family in this beautiful setting and it was perfect. We were gradually putting our lives back together again and transforming in so many different areas, but we were about to discover something that I had been searching for, for years and it would transform my life in so many ways.

# 19
## NEW BEGINNINGS

That trip to Malaysia was a very special time for both of us. When we had our wedding blessed a couple of years earlier, I can remember saying to Cindy on that day that she had been the one who had looked after me for the last twenty years and now it was my turn to look after her. I wanted this trip to be special for her and I know it was but it was also such a wonderful experience for both of us. We landed in Singapore and went to our hotel with a pool on the roof. We put our bags in the room and went down into the street; the first thing we saw was a food hall, a large hall known as 'hawkers'. As you walk in you are hit with the aroma of the local food and that of around the world. I was in heaven and wanted to try them all. After the food, we went back to our room but couldn't sleep. I think we were too excited and the time difference was a factor but we got up and went for a walk and found ourselves eating roti changi at three in the morning and went back to the hotel to sleep.

We spent two nights at the hotel and then met Cindy's sister, Diana and went to stay with her. I was starting to understand that one tradition of Malay and Singaporeans was to always offer food whenever anyone visited them and we would be visiting quite a lot while we were there so I thought it would be rude to say no, or that was my excuse anyway.

Diana was the eldest sister and she would be taking us to Malacca, which is the Portuguese settlement where the three sisters were born: Diana, Hazel and Cindy. We travelled by bus and the journey took about four hours. We stopped halfway for something to eat, and I remember Cindy buying fried bananas and fresh fruit to take back on the bus with us. When we arrived we booked into a hotel called The Pink Hotel. It was a bit run down to say the least but it was next to the settlement where Cindy had been born and once we had booked in we all went to look for the house. Diana is Cindy's oldest sister by twelve years so she can remember more about when they were younger. The houses were bungalows and we walked for a little while until Diana got her bearings and then we found it. I asked Cindy how she felt when she first found the house and she said it was a mixture of excitement and tinged with sadness. The sadness was that she couldn't remember much about being there because she had left when she was about eighteen months old.

We next went to visit some relatives that still lived in the settlement: Auntie Aggi, Uncle Kenneth and Auntie Freda. Freda had been Cindy's mum, Carmen's best friend. This was a chance for Cindy to have some of the blanks filled in for her as they all, including Diana, talked about how it was back then and the memories they had of her mum and especially her dad, who she was too young at the time to remember. Cindy had only heard her mum's version of him that wasn't very flattering due to his philandering when they had been together as a married couple.

That evening, Kenneth and Aggi took us into the harbour area where we had a beautiful meal outside and sat by the sea watching mudskippers as the sun was setting. It was still warm. We stopped late into the evening drinking fresh mango juice. I was feeling even closer to Cindy and full of gratitude; this was a million miles from where I had come and for a while I just bathed in the warmth of those feelings and then it was time to say our farewells and made our way back to The Pink Hotel.

The next morning we would board the bus for our journey back to Diana's house in Singapore and meet more family members and get a chance to explore the city, including a Zoo that was set in the forest with animals running about that appeared to be loose and magnificent waterfalls that were so high you couldn't see the top. This was right up my street and felt like a kid again. It was a fantastic time and I was beginning to see how close those family ties are for Malaysians and saw how Cindy was bringing those traditions into our home. I was able to now appreciate just how important that was.

We had the shock of a lifetime on our second visit to Malaysia a few years later. Cindy had found out from her sister, Hazel that she had other cousins from her father's side of the family living in Kuala Lumpur that she had not yet met. One of these cousin's, Kamiriah arranged a reunion that involved fifty or more family members including Cindy's half-sister, Harietta that she had also never met before. This was not only overwhelming for Cindy, it was for me too. My family consisted of my brother and one cousin that had dropped off the radar and who we couldn't find. At the reunion, I remember that we had to have sticky labels with all our names on in order to remember who everyone was. My job on the night was to record it all on a camcorder and spent most of my time interviewing the guests to find out who they were and who they were related to. They were all happy to take part as they understood that this was a once in a lifetime opportunity. They were also sending love and regards to Cindy's mum who wasn't able to make the journey with us because by this time her age made it too much for her to manage a twelve-hour flight.

On our first trip we had found an island that we just fell in love with called Langkawi and decided to travel there after our trip to Kuala Lumpur. The first time we visited it we stayed at a resort that was owned by another cousin. It was called Tok Senik and it is set in the jungle in traditionally built wooden buildings on stilts called kampongs. We loved it and we were surrounded by wildlife and could hear the troops of monkeys calling to each other. The restaurant was open around the sides and eating breakfast while watching the activities of the surrounding jungle was wonderful. At night, we would get visitors once the light went out and I would often be woken by Cindy shaking me and saying that something was in the room. I didn't think much of it but

I was made to put the light on and go looking for whatever it was. They seemed to like searching in cupboards and we never did see them but it would happen every night. I found it amusing but not so much Cindy.

We hired a little car to explore the island and it was really stunning at that time and by accident we found perhaps one of the most beautiful beaches on the island. It was called Tanjung Rhu and it was stunning. I was now reaping the rewards of the work I was putting into my recovery and at the same time we were healing the wounds of the past.

We eventually had to leave but we took some wonderful memories home with us and I learned a lot about how important family ties are and it helped me realise that building those ties takes effort and commitment. I had been shown something that I would take home with me and work towards myself with Cindy and our family.

I was still early in my recovery, maybe five years at that time but when I say "early in my recovery", I am not talking so much about my addiction. I didn't think about taking drugs; this was all about changing behaviours, negative thought patterns and limiting beliefs that could plague me at times when things weren't working out. I had been trying lots of different ideas over the years. For instance,

NA had introduced me to the importance of journaling and writing about my feelings, about gratitude and not falling into the trap of only focusing on what's wrong in my life. I started to practice prayer and meditation but it didn't come easily to me. By this time, I had worked through the NA Twelve Steps a few times and felt I had some structure and framework to my life that supported me, not just the programme but the fellowship of the people in it. I had found my 'tribe' and at that time it was a bunch of recovering addicts. For a time I thought this was all I would need, a sort of one stop shopping but it wasn't. It was only the beginning of a longer journey. I was starting to realise that I was slowly changing and as the fear of relapsing subsided I was feeling more confident and often felt this journey to be an adventure.

After the Waterways job had come to an end, I went back to college and trained to be a counsellor. It was an Edexcel level 3 Diploma in developing counselling skills. I remember being the only man in the class of about fifteen and they were all a lot younger than me. I know I always felt disadvantaged in these situations due to my lack of any formal education but that never stopped me going after what I wanted or in this case what I thought I wanted.

Time for a new career and by this time Cindy was working in Lynwode Manor, which is a rehab in Lincolnshire but the owner was keen to expand and opened another facility in Barnsley. Cindy was asked to work there as a manager in the enquiries office and I was also offered a job in the enquiries office, where I would basically answer the phone, answer questions and book people in. I was sure this was what I wanted to do and I would get a chance to grow with this new company but eventually I would be disappointed. I would say ninety percent of the staff were in recovery and I had this idea that I was part of this noble cause to help suffering addicts and alcoholics but I started to see another side to it. After a time, I was starting to see the same clients coming back in and it was more about money than recovery. There were some members of the staff that were well-in with the owner who had massive egos and I felt were quite toxic in the way they spoke and how they treated people. The environment was turning sour for me but the owner was determined to open more facilities and was pouring money into new projects in spite of warnings from his accountant. The turning point for me was when I overheard a member of staff saying to someone as he passed the lounge at Barnsley where a few clients were watching television, "When I look in that lounge, I don't see three recovering alcoholics,

I see ten grand." I was shocked and started to see that this wasn't a philanthropist wanting to give back. I now saw it as a 'cash cow', a revolving door that rode on the back of the NA programme by teaching them the first few steps, taking them to a few meetings and putting them back out again to mostly fail. It wasn't just this treatment centre, I found most of them were this way, unfortunately.

I remember one person in particular that had travelled all over the world working in the oil industry as a diver. He had already been through the Barnsley facility once and he had relapsed and his sister had booked him in again and I had been asked to go and pick him up from his home. He was a lovely man but a chronic alcoholic and when I got there he was in a dressing gown and not wanting to go as his sister pleaded with him. I managed to have a chat with him and he agreed to go. We travelled back to Barnsley. He had been in treatment two or three times and the next time I saw his sister was at his funeral after another this time fatal relapse.

There had to be more to addiction than this. I was seeing people get clean and sober and stay that way for a time, sometimes only weeks but others managed years and still went back out there, relapsing and sometimes dying. Funerals were getting more frequent and the reasons that were being given for why this was happening, such as "They weren't ready"; "They didn't want it bad enough"; "They were incapable of being honest" and the list went on but it was wearing thin on me. There had to be an answer and I was searching for it and one day I would find it.

I was about to move again to another new facility in Pickering not far from Scarborough only this time I would need to stay on site and sleep there. Cindy and I had been travelling from Barnsley daily and even though it was quite a way at least we were home every night. This was going to be different and I was going to learn something that was going to lead me towards what I was searching for. I was at Pickering as a support worker but my main job was to keep an eye on the residents during the night. I would stay awake most of the night and catch up on my sleep during the day. I was also doing a correspondence course in drug, solvents and alcohol counselling and my spare time during the day was a perfect opportunity to do this work. I would sometimes help out during the day if there was a new client and they needed to do part of the admission form which was called the 'psycho/social report'. This report would be a breakdown of significant events throughout their lives starting at naught to five and going up in five-year increments until the present time. I was going through this with a particular lady and she was speaking about being abused sexually and physically by her father for a number of years from a young age. She was so distraught as she told me and I really felt for her. When it was over, I took my report to the counsellors to feedback what I had been told by this lady expecting them to decide who was best qualified to work with this client, only to hear them say "Well, we don't want to open that can of worms do we?" and they all agreed. I was shocked but knew in that moment that this is where the answer lies. This is the area that no one wants to look at and so-called professionals are sweeping it under the carpet and setting those clients up to fail and some will lose their lives.

I had already had my own experience of so-called counsellors working with trauma and now these so-called counsellors where I was working were ignoring it altogether; it was time for me to go. I was totally disillusioned with treatment facilities in general and although obviously some people do get clean, I believe it is more luck than judgement. Don't get me wrong, as I have said it wasn't just this facility. This model was the Minnesota Model of Addiction Treatment that was being used nationally and globally in most treatment facilities, even to this day. I am sure some of them have been expanded on since that time to provide more specialist involvement but some I know of still provide only the bare bones, ignore unresolved trauma or have no staff on board equipped or skilled enough to address these areas.

I had made my mind up that I had to go. This is not what I signed up for and with hindsight I was naïve but deep down just wanted to make a difference in someone's life. At the time I was doing three or four nights and then going home for a few days.

On one of those days I was out with my hawk, Leia on some land steeped in ancient folklore called Byard's Leap. The story involved a witch called Old Meg, a Knight and a blind horse called 'Blind Byard'. So anyway, I was out on my own flying Leia when I bumped into an old friend of mine, Jason. All his family had been in construction work and I had worked for his dad and with his brothers before. He also had a Harris hawk that he was flying and we got talking. He told me about a big job coming up at a local power station that would run for four or five years and asked if I was interested. This seemed like an opportunity to earn some decent money, something that I hadn't been able to do the last year or so. Yes, the other downside of working in treatment centres at that time was the wages were minimum. So I told him that I would and he said he would have a word with his dad, Billy. Shortly after that I was told I had the job and I immediately resigned my position at Pickering.

This next job was going to be one of the hardest jobs I had done for quite some time but it was going to be one of the most lucrative in all my years working in construction, and would subsequently lead to being able to make some major changes around the house that we now had a mortgage on. I didn't know it at the time but I was about to start my own business, only before that could happen something else would need to be in place.

What I was about to discover was the missing link that I felt I had been searching for in self-help books, seminars, online courses and programmes for years. I had been looking for this answer for so long and now it was about to be revealed to me. It all started with Cindy and I visiting a local 'Mind, Body and Spirit' event at our local showground. We were frequent visitors to these shows and would listen to the presentations and learn about some of the alternative therapies that were attending. On this particular day, I had found a lady at her stall and she did something called EFT that stood for Emotional Freedom Techniques. I had no idea what it was and had no idea what the techniques were but I saw on her banner what it could help with, and that included anxiety, depression, addictions and unresolved trauma. Now at this point you would think that the penny would have dropped but the first reason I had for speaking to her was that it might be a good technique for my sponsees. I now had four or five sponsees of my own that I was helping to work through the steps.

I had tried a couple of times to speak to her but she was always busy with someone else but this hold up had its uses because during the wait the penny did finally drop and I realised that it may well do me some good. I had been walking around for a while by now without seeing her free to talk to, and I was making my way to the exit and about to give up when I had a feeling come over me that I needed to go back and so I did. When I did get a chance to speak to her I found out she lived in Lincoln, which was only a few miles away from me. I explained to her that I was in recovery and had been for a number of years but was still having problems with bouts of anger and I didn't like some of my behaviours and they don't seem to have changed much from when I was in the madness of active addiction. I also said that I felt that my traumas from the past had always played a part in my problems and she agreed and invited me to book in for some sessions with her and that is just what I did. I had no idea of what a profound effect this decision was going to have on the rest of my life.

I didn't know why I did that on that particular day because although I agreed to sign up to work with this lady, I didn't ask her how it worked or how often I would need to keep seeing her. You might think I was one of these people that just signed up for everything but that was not the case; I was searching for an answer to my problems but I had been coming to places like the Mind, Body and Spirit events for quite some time. I was more than a little sceptical of some of them. This was the first one I had a really strong feeling about and I don't know why but I knew I needed to do this.

I was now working on my new job at Ratcliffe Power Station and so the money wasn't an issue. We always finished work around one o'clock in the afternoon on a Friday, so I set my appointments for every Friday afternoon. What I didn't know was that I was about to be shown something, a simple technique that was going to completely transform my life and those around me forever. New beginnings were on their way.

## 20
## FORGIVENESS IS THE KEY

It came to the day of my first appointment
with Ruth and on the journey to her house my
mind was racing; I wondered what was going
to happen and what we were going to start
with. I arrived at her house that was in a cul-
de-sac in a village on the outskirts of Lincoln.
I walked to the back door and Ruth was there
to meet me and show me into the room which
was quite a large room with a massage-type
table to the left on the back wall, with a high
chair next to it, a fish tank sat against the
opposite wall, with a small table and two
chairs. I was aware of calming music playing
quietly in the background. Our first session
was for an hour and a half and it began by us
sitting at the table while I explained to Ruth
what I was hoping to achieve.

I can remember the feelings of excitement and apprehension at the thought that this could be the answer to my prayers. I had no idea what was about to happen but Ruth explained to me that she would be tapping with two fingers on different parts of my face and body while talking and then showed me where those points were by giving a demonstration. I felt completely at ease as we began. I have no idea what we started working on in that first session but I had told Ruth about my past and I am sure it would have been one of those early childhood traumas. All I do know is when she was finished working on that particular trauma it was gone and if I tried to recall it I couldn't and I felt completely different about it.

I was convinced from the first day that I was in the right place and this is what I had been searching for all these years, and as the weeks went on I was even more convinced. These traumas were melting away like butter on a hotplate. I just found it unbelievable because it wasn't just that the emotional charge connected to that memory that was removed but what really astonished me was if I tried to recall this memory that had been crystal clear to me just before the treatment it wasn't there anymore. I knew it had happened but it was fragmented and hard to put back together. I worked with Ruth for a number of weeks and as time went on I noticed subtle changes in how I felt; I didn't feel so angry, things that had annoyed or bothered me before seemed easier to deal with. I was changing and I could feel it.

Some months earlier while working the NA steps, I was asked to write a 'no-send letter' to my dad and I was to read it out loud at his graveside. I remember reading that letter and how much hate and anger I had towards him in the first part but as I read through it and came to the end of that letter I found myself in floods of tears and telling him how much I loved him, because deep down I knew this was true as I continued this clearing work with Ruth it was allowing me to reconnect with him. I began to have some compassion for this man that I blamed for everything that was wrong in my life. I started to consider where he had come from and how he had been brought up, what he had experienced. He never spoke about his childhood and I wondered if he was maybe as frightened as I had been and just lashing out in frustration at the world. All I do know is I was starting to love that man and knew that he was doing the best he could with what he had. Once that happened, something quite wonderful happened; all the good memories of our times together began to filter to the surface.

I heard this quote and it made so much sense. I don't know who wrote it but it goes like this, " When we forgive we release a prisoner and then we realise that prisoner was us."

I was remembering my dad teaching me how to fish and his sense of humour, how he loved to sit with a pan of fresh peas shelling and eating them, or a steaming pan of Jerusalem artichokes while watching television. I had a picture of him on a motorbike during the war when he was stationed in Jerusalem as a dispatch rider. I remembered going to the pictures with him one night when we were working together on Fiddlers Ferry and seeing a Walt Disney film and both of us were laughing so much we had tears streaming down our faces. These memories and more came back to me and my whole relationship around my dad was changing and I loved it and this was only the beginning.

There was no way I could have known to what extent my life would be changed from these simple but powerful techniques; how the hell could tapping on a few points while talking about my problems have such a profound effect? It wasn't quite as simple as this but in essence this is what EFT was. I didn't miss one appointment, I was hooked and this time it was in a good way. I wanted everything it could offer and as time went on I started to feel more changes taking place, I didn't know what it was called but it was a feeling as if my mind was recalibrating itself. It is hard to explain and some experts call it 'memory reconsolidation' and I think some therapists try to take credit for this process but I came to believe the process to be a natural one. I saw situations that in the past would have had me spitting nails or someone saying something that would cause me to fly off the handle and angrily defend myself by arguing and not being able to let go. I wasn't feeling constantly on guard from some imagined adversary. There was a sense of peace coming over me that I had never felt before, a feeling of being safe for the first time in my life, truly safe. The war really was over for me at last and I could begin to enjoy life.

These changes did not go unnoticed especially by Cindy and the changes didn't happen overnight, I don't want to give the impression it was some sort of magic bullet. A trauma was usually resolved in one or two sessions but the changes happened over a number of weeks. I would just suddenly find myself in a situation that would usually have caused me to blow my top and I wasn't, for instance 'road rage'. I had terrible road rage, and on one occasion on a trip to the local beach in Skegness with all the family on board, a car passed me and then had to cut sharply in front of me to avoid an oncoming car causing me to brake hard to avoid an accident. I suppose I had a good reason to be angry but I didn't just get angry, it was pure rage. I was honking my horn at him and he flipped me the finger and now I was going ballistic. Just as we came around a bend the traffic came to a standstill and in a second I was out the car and pulling at his doors to drag him out but he had quickly locked them when he saw this madman approaching and so I proceeded to kick in all the panels of his car in frustration.

As I went back to the car I could see my family sliding down their chairs in embarrassment as we now had a queue of traffic behind us that had witnessed all that had just happened. I remember Cindy giving me a hard time about it and said "One of these days you are going to meet your match and someone is going to get out their car and give you a good hiding!" I think in that moment she was quite relishing the thought. When I had that rage come over me, I'd never think of the consequences or anybody else, including my family. It really is a blind rage; the red mist comes down and wild horses won't hold me back.

Figure 9 - Cindy & Theresa

The first time I was made aware of how selfish my behaviour could be is when Cindy and I went to see a counsellor at the rehab in Nottingham. Her name was Audrey and she offered to help us with our marriage that we were both struggling with in those early days. We went along and during this particular session she showed me something that was going to shock me and stay with me. She gave me a scenario and in it she said, "If you were out shopping with Cindy and someone knocked her down, grabbed her bag and ran off, what would you do?" Without hesitation I said, "Run after the guy who had stolen the bag" and then she said, "What about Cindy? Is she hurt or injured?" In that moment I suddenly realised how I was more concerned with catching the thief and making him pay or retrieving the bag with her purse in it than tending to Cindy and checking if she was ok. My bruised ego was more important than any injuries or how upset my wife was and it shocked me because in my distorted way of thinking I believed I was doing the right thing and this wouldn't be the first time my belief system was to be challenged.

I was seeing how I had this automatic response to some situations and there was no pause for thought. It wasn't just road rage. There were lots of situations where how I reacted wasn't helpful or healthy and was impacting on so many areas of my life, not least of all my wife and children.

Resolving my traumas was having a profound effect on not only my behaviours but my thoughts and feelings, but I was also aware that I had a lifetime of conditioning and beliefs that were getting in the way of the life I envisioned for me and my family. I had more than hope now, though. I was coming to believe that there was a bright new future in front of us. Let the adventure begin!

While I was still working with Ruth I decided I wanted to train to be an emotional freedom practitioner. This was not something I had any intentions of keeping to myself. I knew there were lots of people just like me that would benefit from EFT and I wanted to give as many people as I could an opportunity to try it. Ruth was also a trainer as well as a practitioner and so I signed up for the Level 1 and Level 2 training that took place over a weekend but the requirement of the second part was finding twenty-five people to work with and produce case studies. Each case study was an hour session and had to be written up afterwards explaining in detail what the issue was and how you worked on it and the result. A lot of the trainees struggled to find twenty-five people to work with but I was fortunate I had my NA members and they were only too pleased to come along and try it out. Let's face it, all recovering addicts have more than their fair share of issues to work on and trauma was always there, so it worked out pretty good because they learned something that they could use themselves for stress, anxiety and other negative emotions. Some even became clients who had realised where their struggles originated and made the decision to work on some of their childhood experiences. I haven't come across one addict or alcoholic that didn't have unresolved traumas, and I am talking about hundreds now!

I mentioned earlier that Cindy had started to notice the changes in me, in fact she was so impressed by what she saw that she did the training too. So, we were now both qualified

EFT practitioners. I later went on to do the advanced training in London and shortly after that started my own business. I had known from those early days that this was not something I was going to keep to myself. I was already telling as many people as possible. It was going to be an uphill struggle as people in general are conditioned to think from a young age that if you are ill, and that includes mental health issues, you go to your doctor and anything else should be treated with suspicion, but thankfully things are changing.

I was still working for Alstom at the power station and at the same time we were making changes to the house. We built an extension on the rear of the house. This was built for the sole reason of having a table big enough for all our family to sit around on Christmas Day! This had been a tradition since I got into recovery and our children had always made that effort to be there, but as the family grew and we started to accumulate more little grandchildren, we needed more space and now we had it. The table had been built by Jack, our youngest son who was building furniture out of reclaimed wood at the time and so we already had a few pieces of furniture in the house built by him. The table is over three metres long and has been well used and not just at Christmas but birthdays, christenings and sometimes just the good old traditional Sunday dinner. One of the reasons we never have a problem getting the kids to turn up on these days is they just love their mum's cooking- it is proper 'soul food'- but it was also an important time for us to be together in our busy lives. For me, it felt like a time for healing. Another contributing factor to all this was after our visit to Malaysia and seeing those strong family ties that were so important to their way of life. I wanted to try and bring it into our lives and those of our children and grandchildren.

Figure 10 - Jack

The family was growing by this time. Theresa had Poppy in 2007 but that relationship Poppy's dad didn't work out and she left him and eventually found Errol and I could see she was happy and I could relax now. Simone had Leo in 2009 and she also left her partner because of how he treated her and what made it worse was that I had no idea how bad it was. Both Theresa and Simone had walked out and left with just their clothes. They have had to start again and they did. I will talk more about this in another chapter as I am starting to get in front of myself.

Jack, by this time had two children- Lillia, born in 2011 and Isabella, born in 2015- and he was living with Flick. I noticed after a while that Jack's behaviour was getting more and more out of hand and I would often get a phone call from Flick in tears and saying how horrible he was being to them all. I recognised these tell-tale signs and feared the worst. I suspected he was using drugs and this time it wasn't cannabis. This was my worst nightmare because I felt responsible but at the same time I couldn't ignore it and hope it went away. I went to his house one day after a call from Flick and confronted him about it. Well, all hell broke loose and although it didn't get physical, it was very close. He was livid and in spite of how scary it was to see him like this, I just saw this younger version of me in how he was reacting to confrontation.

I continued to confront him about his use of cocaine and I knew I couldn't stop him doing it and I had to try and practice unconditional love. The bottom line was that he was my son and I might not like what he is doing but I love him and as he is my son I could never reject him and made the decision that I will be there for him when he is ready. I had a lot of support from Pete (my NA sponsor at that time) and at one point I thought we had turned a corner but he was back at it again and I had no idea until we were on a family holiday shortly after he had proposed to Flick, got engaged and set a wedding day. It was about three days into our holiday in Cornwall when he started being argumentative and wanting to leave. We were trying to talk him out of it and then he just blew his top and said some terrible things and just put the kids and Flick in the car and left. Everyone was so upset but I knew that wasn't him and he must be using drugs again. I suspect he had brought some with him and ran out and then looked for an excuse to leave and, when that didn't work, made it impossible to stay by falling out with everybody. I knew about that behaviour. I had used the same tactics lots of times and then tried to blame everyone else for why it happened. The unfortunate thing was that the wedding was only a few weeks away and nobody wanted to go at that point. We did go and it was a wonderful day and I believe it was a turning point for Jack because he knew we had his back no matter what and just like me he wanted to be a family man. When I was using drugs, the most painful part about it was that deep down I wanted my family to be proud of me but I kept letting them down and that is so painful. I am sure Jack felt that, too.

It was time for me to think about getting my new business started. I was lucky enough to have a friend from NA who was also a graphic designer and helped me set up my first website. This period in my life was a massive learning curve for me. I had to learn so much and build pages for the website, copy and paste stuff, copyright laws. I thought learning how to text and send pictures on my phone was a major achievement, but this felt well out of my comfort zone! Gradually I started to learn more and became more confident. There were times when I would get frustrated, have a tantrum and then want to throw the towel in but I didn't and the thing that motivated me to keep going was that I was passionate about how many people this could help and so I just persevered until it started to all come together.

I started off doing free sessions for friends and family and then gradually I began to pick up a few paying clients. It was early days and I was still learning my trade. I wanted to be the best and so I trained with Master EFT trainers and practiced with lots of people with different challenges, stress, anxiety and depression were the main ones but panic attacks came up quite often and every time we searched for the origins of the original problem usually a trauma would appear. Although I was making progress in my business there was a major setback and that was I was mostly trying to build it during the five or six months when I was not working in my main job. I knew that sooner or later I was going to have to make a decision to commit to the new business completely but I wasn't ready yet and I felt I was still building my skill set and learning to manage and market the new website.

Every year around September, I would start to attract a few clients and work on the website and then as we approached March I would have to scale things down and put it in mothballs until the following September. I had made a decision that I was going to have to let go of this contract work. The truth was I was frightened of letting go of it, not only was it the only thing I had known for most of my working life but another hurdle was letting go of the money. At that time I could earn more than most people earned in a year for six months work; it was a lot to let go of but I knew I would have to do it at some point if I wanted to follow my passion.

Working at the Waterways job had taught me that being valued and enjoying what I was doing is more important than how fat my pay packet was. I also wanted to help other people and I had been shown that being of service to others is a part of what connects us to each other. I don't want to ever forget that because I did forget it for a long time and I definitely wasn't happy.

# 21
## DISCOVERING ACEs

I was coming to the end of my power station work. I would do it by increments over a period of time but I would get there eventually. It had not only become physically too much for me but it had also served its purpose. It had been about the money; money was the main motivation for going to work and now we had built the extension, I had plans for a koi pond. I had my hawk, the all-important table was in the extension for our family get-togethers, I had a nice car and the website was ready to go. Now it was time for me to develop my own business and follow my passion but before that happened I had a chance to get Jack a job with me at Ratcliffe Power Station. It was the penultimate year there, so the work was coming to an end.

When Jack started he had to go on nights to begin with. It was his first time on a site like this and I knew the work was dangerous. I wanted him with me so I could keep an eye on him and make sure he was safe but that wasn't to be. Fortunately, I had a couple of mates, Docker and Bob Griff who were also on nights and they promised to look after him for me. He had stopped using cocaine and he was getting his life back on track so this was an opportunity for him to earn some good money. The lads on nights were telling me how well he was doing and what a good worker he was and I can remember how proud I felt. He wasn't on as much money as the other men because he was classed as a handyman but every week his supervisor would have a collection to make his money up. The night shift didn't last long and he came over to days and we had a chance to work together for a little while, just like I had a chance to work with my own dad all those years ago. It was a special time for me and I am so pleased that I got the opportunity to do it.

We completed the work and after three months of working seven days a week and long hours, it was time for a well-earned rest. This was a time when power station work as I had known it was coming to an end. These old, dirty coal-fired stations were gradually being decommissioned and were slowly disappearing and being replaced with the more environmentally friendly gas-fuelled stations. There was a final year left at Ratcliffe and Jack could have come back that year but once that job ended, everything would change. Finding work would become more difficult and it would have meant living out of a suitcase and travelling all over the country to find work. I knew what that was like and how hard it was on a young family and so he rightly decided to stick with the job he was doing, working with cars for a large company. He was starting to work his way up the ladder and the firm soon saw his potential and they eventually made him a supervisor with his own office. He has excelled beyond their expectations but more importantly, he was valued and he loved the work.

Things were good again. Both Theresa and Simone were happy and getting on with their lives. Simone had worked at the family-run, high-end designer clothing shop owned by my brother and his wife Sarah. They were coming to a time in their lives where they wanted to take more of a back seat in the business and made Henry (their son) and Simone directors. At around the same time, Theresa, who had worked at a hair and beauty salon where she had worked for a number of years, would also be made a director of that company. Cindy and I could relax and feel content and not have to worry about anything. Our children and grandchildren were settled and happy and so were we.

A couple of years ago, Jack and a few friends helped me fulfill another of my dreams and that was to have a Koi carp pond. We hired a mini digger and started work. It would be five feet deep and we would have a wall of railway sleepers around the top to protect the grandchildren from falling in. It has a waterfall and has some lovely fish in it. I am looking at it now as I sit at the big dining table writing and the sound of the water from the waterfall is such a tranquil sound. This is my favourite place to watch the sunrise over the fields at the bottom of the garden.

Over the years I had been introduced to and began studying the 'Law of Attraction'. After watching 'The Secret', I was starting to understand how our thoughts and feelings can influence our lives in so many different ways, both positively and negatively. I began to read more and Bob Proctor was one of the first people I started to follow, together with Dr. Joe Dispenza and Greg Braden. They would talk about energy and vibration and how our thoughts are sending out messages in the form of frequencies into the universe and our lives can be influenced by the thoughts we create, not only externally but also internally. I learned how someone who lives with depression or anxiety over time will be far more likely to suffer physical illnesses and autoimmune illnesses, which are some things that seem to show up on a regular basis.

This isn't the place for me to get into a long discussion on this subject, which is a book on its own. I just started to understand that we are co-creators of our own lives through the quality of our thoughts and feelings. Not only that, but EFT was the ideal natural maintenance tool to ensure I could clear anything that was interfering with my peace of mind. I had learned through EFT that negative emotions or feelings cause a disruption in the body's energy system known as the meridians and by tapping on specific points on the face and body these disruptions could be remedied and we could return to feeling calm and at peace in a matter of minutes. This was nothing new; Chinese medicine had been working with meridians for 5,000 years.

My searching was about to uncover something else that was going to have a major effect on me and put into place the pieces of the puzzle that I had always felt intuitively to be true. I can't remember exactly how I came across it but one day I found something called 'The

ACE Study'. The 'ACE' stood for 'adverse childhood experiences' and was first published in 1997 by Kaiser Permanente and the CDC in America and at the time it was the biggest study of its time, involving 17,337 volunteers from a health organisation. These people were middle class, with jobs, college educated and an average age of 57 years. They were given a thorough medical examination and a questionnaire with ten questions on it split into three categories:

Abuse... emotional, physical and sexual

Household challenges… mother treated violently, household substance misuse, household mental illness, separation or divorce, incarcerated household member

Neglect… emotional neglect and physical neglect.

The outcome of the study showed just how prevalent ACEs were: 67% of those that took part had at least one ACE and 11% had five ACEs or more. It showed that adverse childhood experiences are vastly more common than recognised or acknowledged, and that they have a powerful impact on our adult life some years later.

Someone with 4 or more ACEs was 2,200% more likely to attempt suicide in their lifetime.

I had tried this, and luckily failed, in Bournemouth.

Someone with 6 ACEs or more had a twenty year difference in life expectancy and this was because these unresolved traumas led to depression, suicide attempts, developing heart disease, cancer, stroke, diabetes, liver disease, alcoholism and drug addiction. Addictions, a heart problem, pre-diabetes; these were all things I experienced.

A male child with an ACE score of 6 or more, when compared to a child with no ACEs, was 4,600% more likely to become an injecting drug user sometime later in life. My ACE score was 7 and the outcome was evident.

A study in 2013 of incarcerated males found that ACE scores above 4 to be four times higher than in the general population of males. Prison had become an occupational hazard to me.

These figures are sometimes hard to swallow but this study was done over a twenty year period where the volunteers were monitored and it was also replicated in eighteen other states and had similar results and now studies are happening all over the world including the UK. The Welsh study is particularly interesting and in-depth.

When I first read this study I felt like I had found the 'Holy Grail'. I had already started to understand that our thoughts and feelings can affect us on an epigenetic level meaning that thoughts and feelings have the ability to turn genes on and off (gene expression) thanks to the work of Bruce Lipton. Those same thoughts and feelings if negative can impair our immune system and flood our bodies with cortisol, the stress hormone that leaves us open to infections and illnesses but although those areas are vitally important I was more interested in the addiction aspect of it.

Before I knew anything about recovery or addiction, something deep down inside me, my intuition, told me that there was more to this. There was something inside me that needed pulling out and that reminded me of the time when I was in treatment when we did some art therapy. I remembered doing a picture of myself and it showed my heart with a tiny dot of gold in the centre of it, my hair was flames signifying my anger but inside of me was this ball of black snakes and I was reaching in and pulling them out one at a time and throwing them on the floor. I still have that drawing somewhere but even then I had some awareness of what I needed to do.

So, now I was armed with this new information I decided to try a little survey of my own and as I had lots of friends and people I knew in Narcotics Anonymous, I asked them to fill the ACE Study questionnaire in. I knew that a lot of them had experienced childhood trauma after hearing them share their stories in the meetings. It was no surprise to me when they were scoring eight, nines and tens. I was offering them some free sessions at that time and most of them, like me, had a feeling that this area of their lives was affecting the quality of their recovery. I believed it was the main reason why I was seeing so many recovering addicts doing all that was being asked of them and still relapsing and some dying. I had been to too many funerals and I was convinced that I could make a difference. I was now working with many different types of mental and physical abuse cases and getting some really good results; some of those that took part wrote testimonials for my website, There was only one that took part that relapsed, and the rest were all doing well.

I was still working in construction but now working for a guy in a place called Ketton, near Stamford. It started off as a six-week shutdown during the winter. It was a cement works and just after Christmas the site is closed down to do any repairs that needed doing. It was outside work and the weather wasn't always good to us but it was a welcomed wage just after Christmas as the power station work was virtually non-existent at that time of year. The guy that owned it was a man called Matt Houden, and I can honestly say he was one of the best people I have ever worked for. He had two sons that also worked for him. It was hard work at times but Matt just made working there almost a pleasure. I eventually worked for him full-time for about three years with two friends, Woody and Barney, who I knew from various power station contracts. They lived in Lincoln, which was only a few miles from Newark. Ketton was around forty miles away so we decided to travel together and take turns in driving to save on fuel costs. I had known Woody and Barny for years but now we would mostly work together at Ketton. I enjoyed myself there, but it was impossible to keep both my jobs going at the same time and my own business had now ground to a halt. Matt knew some of my history and what I was trying to do regarding helping others and getting my little business off the ground. He showed a real interest in what I was doing and only too keen to help me, and one day he would prove it.

An NA friend of mine contacted me. He knew about the work I did and in fact, I had helped him with some of his own childhood experiences. His name was Sean Murphy and over time we had become close friends. He was working for the YMCA in Derby at the time and he had become aware that there was some funding available and put my name forward and explained what I did to his managers. I was eventually given a slot one day a week to work with the residents. As I mentioned earlier I was still working for Matt so I went and told him about what I had been offered and he agreed to let me have Wednesdays off. That was just the sort of man he was: generous, kind and supportive.

I enjoyed working at the YMCA and some of those young people I worked with had complex issues and some were heavily medicated but they would still make the effort to come along to the sessions and were making some real progress. They were not only clearing things from their past but also learning how to control their emotions and behaviours by using EFT for themselves. There was so much trauma involved in how these young people's lives were being ruined but I was only there for a few months and sometimes they would be moved on to somewhere else after a couple of sessions and I wouldn't see them again but at least I helped them a little and gave them tools to take away with them. Sean moved on to a new job and shortly after that, the funding ran out and so did my time there. It had been a good experience for me even though the facility had limited space and resources.

There would come a time when I would have to make a decision and finally bite the bullet. Matt had been really good by letting me have days off to do the work I was picking up and although I was doing intermittent work for him and trying to make the final break, I was still coming back every now and again for a week or two on a shutdown to build up my finances. Matt would always give me a ring if he had any work available and that meant a lot to me. I know even now if I rang him and said I needed to earn some cash he would find me something. Working for someone like Matt was a far cry from what I was used to on the power stations where you really were just a number and supervisors and management had very little respect for their workforce. Matt was different but eventually I had to leave. I had to make that break and concentrate on my real passion and that was my new business. I had called it Real Changes for Life because I knew that this is just what it can offer.

I had also realised that this wasn't just about addictions and that it would help anyone who wanted to thrive and improve their physical health, careers, relationships, mental wellbeing, personal growth and so much more. I was starting to attract people who were trapped in the past and had symptoms such as stress, anxiety, depression and panic attacks. These symptoms were showing up in their lives and the only thing that was available to them at the time was a doctor prescribing antidepressants or some other drug.

I was beginning to understand that all these people were no different to me. They had symptoms that were being treated with drugs and it made no difference if the drugs came from a doctor or off the street, they were still drugs and because the root cause of the problem was never looked at, then they just prolonged the problem and in a lot of cases made things worse.

The ACE Study had opened my eyes to all this but I had been looking at it from an addiction perspective and now I was seeing that this was much bigger and far more prolific than an addiction problem.

I was seeing more and more, mostly women that were tired of taking prescription drugs and were desperate to find another way. I loved it when they realised just like I did that EFT (this strange tapping thing) could change their lives.

I began this journey thinking I just needed to stop taking drugs and everything else would just fall into place but it was so much more than that and I was now seeing the bigger picture as more and more people contacted me without an addiction but all the symptoms of unresolved trauma. I had a new group to work with and help.

This transition of building my business without the safety net of a wage coming in wasn't easy for me and I had a real fear that I wouldn't survive financially. I was so used to earning a certain amount of money every year and now this would be gone and replaced by my state pension that barely covered my bills. I know I had a scarcity mentality when it came to money and believe me I was working on it.

I haven't mentioned this before but throughout the time between learning about EFT and now, I had been using it on myself as a maintenance tool for all sorts of issues that would surface from time to time and scarcity being only one of them. Stress and anxiety would still invade my world every now and then and now that I am out of my comfort zone they are even more active. So using the skills I had learned would help me to not become trapped by fear. I was constantly challenging myself to try new things and EFT was the tool that would calm my fears and allow me to keep moving forwards. If I allowed fear to take over I would grind to a halt and never reach my goals. I had the usual suspects in tow, "You're not good enough, smart enough, you're too old to start a business, who do you think you are?" The list goes on. These are nothing more than beliefs that have been imprinted on me from other people and it was my job to remove them. There is something that Gary Craig the founder of EFT developed called the 'Personal Peace Procedure' in EFT, where you list all the areas of your life that are limiting you or holding you back in some way and use the tapping to release them one at a time and that's what I did. I found this an amazing way to free up some space in my internal hard drive that was slowing me down or even keeping me stuck at times spinning my wheels. I would highly recommend this technique to anyone.

I had resolved the traumas from my past and was feeling the benefits of that; now it was time to sift through what was left. I came to learn that all limiting beliefs came from other people. It was time for a massive spring clean of all the misinformation I had accumulated over the years and I would do a little bit every day and just chipping away and finding not only a little more freedom but uncovering who I really was. I had been seen as many things by many people and I had played different roles, but in all that madness I had truly lost myself. I had been living under a false identity and now was the time to confront the imposter and find out who I truly am. This part of the process might be time consuming but I embrace the task at hand because guess what, I am starting to like the person I am discovering stripped of masks and everything else I hid behind. Free at last!

Life was ticking along nicely when I got a bit of a health scare. I had gone along to my favourite restaurant, The Friendly Farmer for a full English breakfast and no sooner had I finished it than I started to feel really strange and I knew something was wrong so I jumped in the car and took myself off to the hospital. By the time I got there which was only a couple of miles I was feeling better and as I stood in the reception area of the A&E. I was on the point of leaving but I went to the desk and told the receptionist what had happened and she advised I just have check-up just to be on the safe side, so that's what I did and the next minute I am in an ambulance with the lights flashing on my way to King's Mill in Mansfield with a suspected heart attack.

I was examined and told I had had a heart attack and I would need to have a stent fitted and that happened the following day. I was then given about five or six types of medication that included statins, blood thinners, beta-blockers, and something to reduce blood pressure. I later found out it wasn't a heart attack as such but a scare, which was a temporary blockage in an artery that cleared itself. I had been taking the medication for a few days but I wasn't happy about it because I had not taken any sort of medication for years and had even avoided having the flu jab.

I made a decision that I would stop all this medication and change my lifestyle regarding eating more healthily and exercise; I also purchased a blood pressure monitor and a glucose and cholesterol testing kit. I went back to see the consultant for a check-up and explained what I had done and read the riot act and was told in no uncertain terms that I would be back in the hospital within two years and this time I was not going to be so lucky. I was told that statins were the only way to reduce my cholesterol levels that by the way were only slightly elevated and that lifestyle changes would make very little difference.

What amused me was that on the first morning after my operation at the top of the menu for breakfast was a Full English. I mentioned it to the nurses when they came round that morning and asked if they were serious. This was probably the main reason I ended up here in the first place. It seems that according to their thinking you could eat what you wanted as long as you take your statins. There was a guy in the bed opposite me that was fairly young and was waiting for a triple bypass surgery, there he was happily tucking into his Full English breakfast. It made no sense to me and I decided to stick to my guns and I am still here alive and kicking, some four years later at the time of writing.

My quest to stay healthy has taken me to try lots of different and sometimes controversial remedies. I have been juicing for some time and bought one of those bullets and made loads of veggie and fruit smoothies. I suffer from stiffness in my joints that I could put down to wear and tear but I think it was more to do with living in a state of constant stress for all those years and the inflammation created by a continuous stream of stress hormones attacking them. There were times when I could only come down the stairs like a crab, sideways.

Before I go into some of the things that I have used I need to say that I am in no way recommending these remedies to anyone they are just what I have found to be useful for myself. I use a number of different things for my joints; turmeric is good and I take it daily. Cindy uses it in her food a lot and I have sometimes added it to smoothies. I use organic apple cider vinegar (Braggs) with bicarbonate of soda to manage my blood sugar levels and it's good for other things too. I use something called MSM that stands for methylsulfonylmethane, which is a natural sulphur containing a compound found in plants, animals and humans. It's widely used for joint pain, reducing inflammation and boosting the immune system. I use large doses of vitamin C, 2000 mg especially if I have been around people with colds and neither Cindy nor I have had a cold or flu for years and we also never take the flu jab. We take vitamin B complex and I also use DMSO at 70% as a spray on my joints; the FDA also frowns this on. I have a shoulder problem at the moment that it is really helping me with. I don't go to doctors unless it is an emergency; I just prefer to use alternative medicines and don't get me wrong I am not anti-NHS, if I have an accident and need to go to the hospital there is nowhere else I would rather be. I am happy for them to put me back together. I just don't want them taking me apart.

I am now officially retired from the construction industry and can devote my time to what I really wanted to be doing and that is building a business and helping as many people as possible. I was relying on word of mouth and that's fine but it wasn't consistent, so the results were sporadic. I was networking locally and visiting a couple of rehabs in the area. One of these rehabs was a charity that was managed by recovering addicts that I knew from the NA meetings, I had sent some information in advance on what I had discovered regarding the ACE study. I had even sent copies of the questionnaire for them to do a little survey of their own. I was invited up for a chat but when I got there and started talking to them, I realised I was wasting my time. The reason was that those that were running the facility had filled out the questionnaire and scored high as was to be expected and even talked about how their behaviours were causing problems with their children and partners but there was no way that I was going to be allowed to work with the clients in those premises because it would mean the staff having to look at some areas of their own lives, too. I can only imagine that it felt threatening in some way to them. I know that most people in these fellowships think that it is some sort of 'one-stop shopping' and that it provides everything they need but that is a misconception that can have dire consequences and does so for so many people.

I must admit that these responses weren't too much of a surprise to me. After all, unresolved trauma had been the elephant in the living room regarding addiction recovery for the last twenty or more years. Let's be honest, to address it would be costly and time consuming especially using the conventional therapies that were available at that time. I even went to a more established treatment facility in Nottingham that had originally been started by a good friend of mine, Tony who unfortunately is no longer with us. I made an offer and went through the procedures that also involved answering questions from a clinical psychologist, which I did do. After all this, it got to the last hurdle which was a board of people I never actually saw and I was simply told what I wanted to provide was not in their remit. I seemed to be hitting brick walls and the sad thing was as long as there are powers that continue to say "No" to trying something different then those that needed what was on offer would suffer, and some will die. I truly believed that as I had watched it happen around me for a number of years. I believe in what I do and I know it works and I am not the only one out there but only a few are trauma-informed but that is improving, thank goodness.

There was something else that I needed to take into consideration and that a lot of these organisations, especially the charities, were relying on funding and it was being reduced all the time, so the money they had available was always going to be an issue.

I was going to have to learn a new strategy to promote what I was doing. I needed a better way to market myself. I wasn't going to be able to help people if they didn't know who I was, what I did and where to find me. It was time to invest in myself with some expert outside help; it wasn't going to be cheap but it was going to be so worthwhile. In the meantime, Sean (my good friend from NA) was about to introduce me to someone who would leave a lasting impression on me.

## 22

## THE PAST IS NOW JUST A STORY

I had a naïve idea that when I started showing people what I had discovered that they would inundate me with requests to come and talk to them about it but that was not the case and I soon realised that change never comes easily or quickly and this was going to take time and persistence.

I held on to Arthur Schopenhauer's quote, "All truth passes through three stages. First, it is ridiculed. Second, it is violently opposed. Third, it is accepted as being self-evident." I was coming to the conclusion that I was not prepared to put any more time or energy in trying to change the minds of those that had a vested interest in maintaining the status quo. I needed to concentrate on where I could be of the most use. I had passion and purpose in my life and I was determined to make a difference and not squander it.

I was being a lot more proactive to promote what I was doing by attending a local business club, attending different colleges on mental health days and I had been invited to speak at an 'EFT Gathering' which was a sort of conference for EFT Practitioners from all over the UK and abroad. I was invited twice to speak there and the second time Cindy was invited to give her perspective on living with an active drug addict. I did a slot on our local radio that was having weekly talks on mental health issues. I had also been invited to speak at the United Kingdom/European Symposium on Addictive Disorders, UKESAD. This was the largest conference regarding addiction and recovery in the UK. This was a massive opportunity.

Unfortunately I had been asked to fill in for someone who couldn't attend and only had about a week to prepare but in spite of the short notice I managed to put a presentation together and had some good feedback from some of the other delegates. I was glad I had Cindy with me who had come along to give me some moral support and I remember spending some time before I went on stage in a toilet cubicle tapping on myself to calm my nerves.

There came a point where I had to just stop and ask myself what I was doing and what my intentions were around this business of ours because it seems that the purpose of it was getting murky and things were changing. I felt I had a conflict and it was that when I thought of becoming successful and that it would feel that it was more about making money than my main reason which was to help as many people as possible. I needed to find a way to find a balance between finding a fair exchange of my time for money and still being able to serve anyone who really wanted help. Most of the addicts that I had worked with didn't have a pot to piss in or a window to throw it out of. I saw that a lot of the help available was expensive and in most cases ineffectual. I wanted to be able to help not just addicts but anyone who needed help. Help shouldn't be only available to those that could afford it but the bills had to be paid somehow. I still had a full time job at that time and it wasn't a problem to me if someone needing help was strapped for cash. This was going to change when I retired so I needed to make plans for the future. One day, someone said something to me that I hadn't thought of and that was 'What if becoming successful meant that the money earned would allow you to help more of those who couldn't pay?". This made sense to me and I now had a different mindset that said the more successful I was the more people I could help. I could relax and get on with learning more about what I needed to do to achieve this. I didn't enjoy learning about online marketing but I needed to and my little business began to grow.

One day, my friend Sean contacted me. He was now with a firm that worked with people who had recently offended and it is called NACRO. He told me they had a young man in their care that was suffering with PTSD and they were concerned about moving him into his own place and would I come over and work with him. I agreed and this case is one that will always stay with me this is how it went...

When I was first approached about this young man, I was told that he had witnessed his friend's murder in the bedsit he was living in and as a result he was behaving in a way that was causing concern to the staff where he was a resident. When we eventually started working on the trauma we used a technique that was very gentle and we just took it very slowly. He would sometimes turn up drunk after being up all night with his friends and smoking cannabis. We reached an agreement that he would at least try and not drink and use drugs the night before our appointment, so that we didn't have to cancel them and he kept to his promise.

The results were this, as we began to work through the murder of his friend, I started to notice over time a change in his appearance, his track suit went, he was wearing clean clothes, he had a haircut and he was sitting up and making eye contact. We moved on to the court case and the traumatic memories he had of that. The changes were not just visible to me but the staff were also making comments on the changes not only in his appearance but in his attitude and behaviour.

We were talking one day and he told me that he was on a warning for attacking a fellow resident after an argument. He told me that he had been punching walls and smashing things in his bed sit, out of frustration and uncontrollable anger for quite some time but that he was not having those feelings anymore. He was so proud when he told me how he had found himself in a situation with a resident that had made him angry but that he was able to say how he felt without losing his temper and put a boundary down. He also said that he had been afraid to go out of the house and the reason that he always had people in his room was that he was frightened to be alone. He said he now enjoyed walking by the local canal and had joined a local gym. There were quite a few other areas from his childhood that we worked on also but he was a wonderful young man.

One day he asked me if he could work on some past family issues because he wanted to have a better relationship with his father. His father had introduced him to cannabis when he was 14 years old and he had continued smoking it from then on but he had recently started rebuilding a relationship with his father and they were going on holiday together. He wanted to clear some of the negative memories he had around his dad before they went. I nearly gave up on this young man in the beginning but I am so glad that I didn't. I had never mentioned his drug use. It wasn't what I was there to help him with but in our last session he said to me out of the blue, "I don't want to use cannabis anymore". I had only been given a glimpse of this young man but I will never forget him as he was a testament to how the negative behaviours become redundant once the trauma is resolved. The trauma is the driving force behind the behaviour, the internal chaos quietens the nervous system, recalibrates itself and there is nothing left to react to.

As I became more adept at marketing my business, mostly through Facebook Ads. I had a surprise coming because I had thought that I would be working people with addictions but I was being contacted more often by people who were saying to me they didn't have an addiction but they do have unresolved trauma and most of the other symptoms such as anxiety, depression, angry outbursts, feeling unsafe, suicidal at times and being on constant alert. These were mostly female and of various ages and backgrounds but recognising what I was saying in the ads regarding feelings and behaviours. I was being shown another group of people that needed help and when I tweaked my advert to speak to this group of people things really took off to the point that I needed to switch one of the adverts off because I had too many clients; a luxury dilemma for me.

This was my new trade and as I began to hone my skills, and add new ones to them, I was seeing how I could help people by passing those skills on so that they could heal themselves. I didn't see myself as a therapist but more of a coach, teaching life skills. The clients learn the skills that can be tools they can use throughout their lives.

I had gradually started to move away from Narcotics Anonymous for various reasons but I had been doing service for that fellowship for ten-plus years and so I think it was time for someone else to have a turn. I was trying different sorts of meditation such as guided ones, chanting and Shamanic to name a few. I was also following different teachings from people like Wayne Dyer, Greg Braden, Dr Joe Dispenza, Joe Vitale and Bruce Lipton. These were all authors and speakers that were talking about the same thing regarding energy and the power of thoughts and feelings and how we are co-creators of our reality.

I feel that I have been on a search for my spiritual path maybe all my life but now I felt I was looking in the right places. My beliefs are based on my experiences so I believe that if we are trapped by the past and looking for things outside ourselves to ease the pain of that, then we will only get fleeting glimpses of what and who we could really be. I know now we are all connected. Being disconnected is not only an unnatural state of being but an extremely painful place to be. I also believe we have an innate ability to heal ourselves. I believe what the new sciences are saying about us being energetic beings swimming in a sea of information filled with infinite possibilities. My definition of spirituality is having a deeply held belief that we are inextricably connected to each other by something greater than ourselves.

There is a book called 'A Course in Miracles' by Dr. Helen Schucman and although I haven't gone through the course I pick it up every now and again and have a read. It talks about love and fear; that fear is created in the mind and love is God given. I believe that fear resides in my mind and love resides in my heart because I feel it, and the magnetic energy field that surrounds the heart is far greater than the mind or the body. I used to think the heart was just a pump for the circulation of my blood but I know now it is far more than that and I learned there is a constant stream of information going on between the heart and the brain. There is far more information coming from the heart to the brain than in the other direction and if the two are in harmony with each other every part of the mind and body will synchronise and we will be performing at our optimal level.

Some days it is hard to understand how I managed to survive those earlier years but I never forget how fortunate I am and the list of those I knew who didn't make it is a constant reminder of that.

I am lucky to have Cindy in my life for so many reasons but one of those reasons is her sense of adventure. She loves fishing and camping when it is warm and we have been on quite a few trips around the country but on one occasion when I was still involved with Narcotics Anonymous, I heard that there was going to be a world convention in Barcelona and suggested we do a road trip and she agreed. We loaded the car up with camping and fishing tackle and set off on our adventure. We had a RAC guide that showed all the camping sites on our route and we circled all the ones that had fishing and just took our time working our way to the foot of the Pyrenees, stopping at beautiful little campsites, fishing and eating and then on to the next stop before our trip up the mountain road with its sharp bends, steep climbs and sheer drops, but also the breathtaking views. Unfortunately, Cindy saw very little of those views in spite of me insisting that she really needed to see this, she continued to keep her eyes covered or looked in the opposite direction, she was so frightened of heights. When we reached the top of the mountains we booked into a hotel as a bit of a treat and discussed the rest of our journey. During the night we had decided that we had had such a good time that we would go back down the mountain back into France and continue our fishing and camping adventure. The NA convention in Barcelona would have to manage without us that year. So, the next morning we travelled back down the mountain and as we did we went by Andorra and saw all these people milling about and wondered what the attraction was, oblivious that it was tax free haven attracting millions of shoppers from all over Europe. Oh well, not to worry, we had more important things on our minds like a campsite with a lake and some big fish to catch. I am so glad we did this together and we had a wonderful time and I was full of gratitude for this new way of living that was so far from where we had come. It really felt as if the universe was conspiring to provide what we needed and we embraced every moment.

Figure 11 - Theresa, Cindy & Simone

The holiday came to an end but not the adventures as we continue to have new ones and our family was growing. Theresa had Poppy, Simone had Leo, Jack had Lilia, Isabella and the newest addition Myah. Steven and Jane from my first marriage had two each; Steven had Josh and Faith, and Jane had Harry and Kate. I didn't see Jane and her family very often as they lived in London but Kate comes over to visit when she can. Steven lives in Newark and so we see him and the family more often.

I learned a lot about family ties from Cindy's family, they will go to great lengths to show up for a family event and sometimes travel from the other side of the world to be there. This was more to do with the Malaysian culture that I warmed to and continued to encourage our own growing family and it is happening but on a smaller scale. We have become a family that will always try and have a get together whenever we get a chance. Barbeques in the summer, picnics, Sunday dinners, camping trips, fishing trips to teach the grandchildren how to fish. I think they have all been at least once, except Jane's children in London. Christenings are always a good reason for us all to get together and so are weddings and our most recent one was about to happen…

Theresa and Errol had been engaged for a while and now had come the time that they decided to tie the knot. The wedding was to take place in France where Errol had converted a barn in a small pretty village into a beautiful house and in the grounds were the ruins of the original stone built house with a massive fireplace and this is where the ceremony took place. Some of us arrived a few days early to help with the preparations and I decided to drive there and yes, you have guessed, with the camping and fishing tackle in the back. Cindy and I were going to have another little adventure after the wedding.

The wedding was a wonderful affair. Errol had gone to great lengths to ensure it would be the perfect day that my daughter would forever remember. We had a few laughs getting it ready and one of the standing jokes was his obsession with the swag on voile drapes in the marquee. His best man, Aidie and I would rib him about it and it even made its way into my speech.

Figure 12 - Simone, Cindy & Theresa

The other guests arrived including my son, Steve and his family. Steve and Theresa had always been close and now he was here and Faith was going to be a bridesmaid along with Poppy and Lillia. Jack was there and my brother, Alan and his family. It was an amazing time.

It came to the day and I went to pick my daughter up from the hotel where she had stayed without Errol. We waited until everyone had left and then Cindy came down with her and she looked stunning. I was trying to hold it together but I just felt so emotional. I had a million thoughts going through my mind at that time but the main feeling was that I was so proud. Here I was totally present and feeling every emotion and it was truly amazing.

We got to the house and I waited for my cue to walk her down to where the ceremony would take place in front of the ancient ruin and as I walked with her on my arm I thought my heart would burst through my chest I was so proud. I stood with Cindy as we watched our daughter being married by the lady minister, we were both so happy. Just as Errol had planned and worked so hard to achieve, it went perfectly, followed by the celebrations that went on for a couple of days. People headed home and then Cindy and I went on another little adventure before heading home ourselves.

It was only a couple of months later that we would be having another big celebration. It was Cindy's mum's ninetieth birthday party in the same year, the birthday party that she was adamant she didn't want. It was organised with all the stealth and secrecy of a well-planned Special Forces operation. She had no idea about it but she finally arrived and came into the room and the look of shock on her face was a picture. People had come from all over the country to be there but after the initial surprise of seeing us all there she had a second surprise when Diana, one of her daughters walked into the room. Diana had travelled from Singapore with her daughter, Sabrina. We have a photo in our front room of that night and it is of Mum with all of her six daughters around her; Diana, Hazel, Cindy, Sandie, Margie and Marina. This was the first time they had all been in the same place at the same time. We also had videos sent from different parts of the world with cousins, nephews and nieces who couldn't make it and projected them onto a wall so Mum could see them all. It was a wonderful evening and although Mum was reluctant to come to begin with we could see how thrilled she was that night and at the end she spoke to us all on the microphone and thanked us all and said how happy she was to have all her daughters around her and finished off with "If I popped off tomorrow, I would die happy".

That day came around too soon for all of us and it was just after her ninety-first birthday that Carmen (Mum) passed away at home after a short illness. We were all there with her at the end including five of the six daughters, one daughter had been to stay with Carmen when she was first taken ill but had reluctantly needed to return home to Australia because of work commitments. When Mum took ill, Marina had travelled from Australia to come and stay with her mum and when she had to leave then Diana, the eldest daughter came from Singapore and stayed. The rest of the sisters would take it in turns to stay with Diana also.

We would all pop in every day to see Mum, she was never alone and when it was close to the end we were all around her bed talking to her, telling her how much we loved her, holding her hand, praying and at the end as she took her last breaths all the sisters surrounded her with love. This beautiful lady who had been through so much but lived her life with dignity and grace passed on to meet all her friends and relatives that were waiting for her in another life. Although that was such a sad time for everyone, especially the sisters, they all supported one another and I was there to support Cindy who was especially close to her mum. She would go to see her mum every Tuesday evening after work to have tea with her. Every couple of weeks, she would go shopping with her on a Saturday and sometimes go to Nottingham and visit the Chinese supermarkets to get sauces and spices for all traditional Malaysian food she was famous for cooking.

Whenever I visited Mum there was always food available and another tradition was New Year's Eve. We would eat a chicken dish called 'curry devil'. I remember how I struggled with the spicy Malaysian food at first but not anymore. Cindy had picked up all her mum's cooking skills and even today she will cook one of Mum's dishes and we eat it off Mum's plates that we brought from her house. I have lots of happy memories about Carmen and we often laugh about was that every Christmas I would get a present from Mum and whatever it was, it was a gauge of if I was in her good books or not. One year, I received a Hawaiian shirt and the following year a matching bag. It wasn't always clear why I wasn't in her good books but it wouldn't take much and it did make us laugh.

The day of the funeral came and as you can imagine Cindy was struggling to contain her emotions but I think the sisters were finding strength in each other. After the funeral, we all went to a reception hall to eat and drink and swap stories of Carmen.

It had been a tragic time but there were so many wonderful memories and we started to realise how fortunate we were that we had that time with her, that the grandchildren had all managed to visit her during the early part of Mum's illness and that the sisters had been able to be with her until the end because it wasn't many weeks later that we were on the Coronavirus lockdown and none of that would have been possible.

Mum had a little garden at the back of where she lived and it was full of plants. In fact, she was so good at caring for plants that if anyone had one that wasn't doing very well they would bring it to Mum and she would revive it. Amongst the plants were lots of ornaments, fairies and small animals and the grandchildren took some little things and built their own little memorial gardens at home to remember her by.

Well, I am reaching the end of this book and I am looking at what I hoped to achieve by writing it. There are a number of reasons but my main reason was to show that no matter how far you fall or what you have experienced and how totally lost you might feel, there is always HOPE! Nobody is beyond hope. I was told over and over again that I was a lost cause but they were all wrong!

I wanted three things after I got clean; firstly, I wanted to become a family man, reliable, loving and someone my family could be proud of. Secondly I wanted to uncover who I truly was, these were always my primary goals, and lastly I wanted to take everything I had learned over the years and teach it to people who are struggling and lost in their own lives and searching for answers. Today I have a life that is beyond my wildest dreams and you can have one too. So, what is next? Simone, our youngest daughter has recently become engaged and we are all really excited about it. We have another wedding on the way and another family celebration. Her fiancée, Henry is a wonderful young man. All our children are happy and settled. What more could we ask for? I can't wait to walk my final daughter down the aisle. I am so lucky.

In the meantime, I am hoping the campsites will start opening up and the little vintage VW campervan we invested in will be loaded up with fishing tackle and grandchildren very shortly for some new adventure.

My past really is just a story but the adventures never end.

# AFTERTHOUGHTS

What if?....Why me?....If only…. Blah! Blah! Blah!

What if my life was predestined?

What if every part of it was to bring me to this time and place?

What if everything I have experienced was a life lesson, an important life lesson?

So that being said, I chose my parents well, they taught me well and equipped me with what I would need to survive the difficult journey that was the first half of my life. It was going to be an endurance test and my dad taught me well about endurance. My mum showed me her indomitable spirit and strength. She also got on her knees and taught me to fight. These were invaluable tools for the treacherous road ahead.

Now the war is over and I am back home, so to speak. Now is the time to turn those things I learned around and use them for good and let go of anything that isn't serving that aim. None of this was wasted; I am who I am not in spite of it but because of it.

When I see my life this way there is no blame, no shame, there are no victims and there was always a greater purpose to it all.

Namaste.

# RESOURCES

I have put together here a collection of some of the books that have made a real impact on me and helped me understand the new sciences and how energy work is the answer to much of the suffering in the world. The world is at last waking up to the chaos that surrounds us and is realising there has to be another way.

A link to the ACE study done in Wales is a good start that not only lists the ten questions but explains what the results of the score mean. Find it here: https://bit.ly/2JfDWSw

'When The Body Says No' by Gabor Maté, MD. The cost of hidden stress. Gabor explores how hidden stress in the body is responsible for so many physical illnesses and he shows case study after case study to support his findings.

'The Biology of Belief' by Bruce Lipton PhD. This book will forever change your mind about the power of your own thoughts. The new science of epigenetics from a cell biologist.

'The Tapping Solution' by Nick Ortner is a solid introduction to Emotional Freedom Techniques. This book then became one of the first documentaries I saw on the subject and can be watched free now. Find it here: https://www.thetappingsolution.com/free-screening/main-2.php

Nadine Burke Harris's presentation on the ACE Study is still one of my favourite TED talks. It is called 'How childhood trauma affects health across a lifetime'. Find it here: https://www.ted.com/talks/nadine_burke_harris_how_childhood_trauma_affects_health_across_a_lifetime?language=en

This is only a small collection of what helped me on my quest to uncover the secrets to living a life in harmony with nature and in an atmosphere of peace and joy.

If you feel you have questions, or you want to know more why not visit my website https://www.realchangesforlife.co.uk/ or join me on my private Facebook group. Find it here: https://bit.ly/3m3sXtD

I look forward to your questions and have a look at the free demonstrations.

# A GIFT...

For all those of you who have read this far,
thank you. There's no better way to say it than
by passing on my mum's famous coconut tart
recipe:

PASTRY

180g plain flour

20g icing sugar

100g cold butter (cubed)

1 egg yolk

1 tbsp of cold water

FILLING

50g unsalted butter (melted and cooled)

2 tbsp caster sugar

1 egg lightly beaten

2 cups desiccated coconut

METHOD

Grease 2 x 12 hole tart tin.

Place flour, sugar and butter in a food processor. Process until it resembles breadcrumbs. Add egg yolk and water and blend until mixture comes together to form a ball. Wrap in cling film and refrigerate for about 30 mins.

Roll out pastry, using a 6.5cm round cutter, cut our 24 rounds of pastry.

Line prepared tart pan with pastry and spoon 1 tsp raspberry jam into each round.

To make coconut topping, combine all ingredients in a bowl and mix together. Spoon topping evenly over each tart.

Bake in a moderate oven (180c) for about 20 mins.

# About the Author

**Trevor Tacey** lives in a village called Kelham on the outskirts of Newark in Nottinghamshire. Trevor is the founder of Real Changes for Life where he helps people overcome life limiting behaviours and more with the same natural drug free techniques that transformed his life.
**www.realchangesforlife.co.uk**

Printed in Great Britain
by Amazon

29630717R00205